DR LUCIE POIRIER

REMEMBER DANIEL

And don't forget the Days of Noah

REMEMBER DANIEL:
And don't forget the Days of Noah

Copyright © 2024 **Dr Lucie Poirier**

ISBN (Paperback): 978-1-964494-32-6
ISBN (Ebook): 978-1-964494-33-3

Printed in the United States of America.

PROMINENT
BOOKS
EDGE

5830 E 2nd St, Ste 7000 #9983
Casper, WY 82609
USA

CONTENTS

CHAPTER ONE

THE PROPHET DANIEL'S CIRCUMSTANCE

A Time in Life

In the third year of the reign of Jehoiakim king of Judah....

—Daniel 1:1 KJV

TIME! THERE ARE a few ways of looking at time. One definition given by the Oxford English Dictionary is "the indefinite continued progress of existence and events in the past, present, and future, regarded as a whole." Another definition on Google is "a point of time as measured in hours and minutes past midnight or noon."

With this in mind, let's talk about "a time in life" for Daniel that would satisfy both of these definitions.

The prophet Daniel was born around 620 BC, which was about 600 years before Christ, and lived until 538 BC, or 538 years before the birth of Jesus. During his teen years, Daniel was taken into captivity to Babylon, about 500 miles from his native land, Jerusalem. In 605 BC while Daniel was still a teen, God gave Nebuchadnezzar, the Assyrian king, permission to overtake Jerusalem. This must have been quite "a time in life" for Daniel.

The book of Daniel is very powerful in that it is prophetic, although it can be difficult to understand. My goal in this book is to make it very simple yet give you a great understanding of it.

In this first chapter, we will look at Daniel's life. Why? I believe we live in a time when our lives, for those of us that are Christians, will have to almost match his way of living.

Daniel was no ordinary person. During his life he seemed to have gleaned the principles of God in a very special way during his generation. Daniel lived and fell into captivity during a time when his nation was very rebellious and wicked. Evidently, he must have been inspired by some holy people. But who were they?

Daniel was born during the time of King Josiah, who became the king of Judah at the age of eight. We learn that he was one of the few good kings for Judah.

King Josiah was well known for raising money to repair the temple of God. He also called a national repentance for God's people. His story is found in 2 Kings 22–23 and in 2 Chronicles 34–35. During King Josiah's reign, Judah was shaken to its knees by an awakening of the God of Israel. Hilkia the high priest and Shaphan found and read God's scroll of laws to King Josiah, and Josiah tore his clothes in repentance. Josiah was in great repentance when he found out that God was angry with Israel. He realized that the generations past were not listening to God and were serving idols.

King Josiah's Effect in Daniel's Life

Daniel was a boy when God shook Israel. Of course, all these events must have made national news. Every household in Jerusalem must have known of this eight-year-old who was made king and then at an appointed time, raised money to repair the temple, found the laws of God, and afterward called for a national repentance. I imagine Daniel's young heart was taking it all in.

I also imagine that Daniel grew up with a mindset that young people can make a difference. After all, this childhood king started at a very young age and made a big impact in the temple of God.

PROPHET JEREMIAH'S EFFECT IN DANIEL'S LIFE

Daniel must have also been inspired by Jeremiah. During that time in life, Jeremiah was the main prophet over Judah. He had begun to prophesy during the thirteenth year of King Josiah's reign and continued as the prophet over Judah all through the reign of King Jehoiakim until the eleventh year of King Zedekiah, the last king of Judah.

> *The words of Jeremiah the son of Hilkiah, of the priests that were in Anathoth in the land of Benjamin: To whom the word of the Lord came in the days of Josiah the son of Amon king of Judah, in the thirteenth year of his reign. It came also in the days of Jehoiakim the son of Josiah king of Judah, unto the end of the eleventh year of Zedekiah the son of Josiah king of Judah, unto the carrying away of Jerusalem captive in the fifth month.*
>
> Jeremiah 1:1–3

God called Jeremiah to be a prophet to Israel and Judah while he was quite young. We know this because his very excuse to God was that he was too young. Daniel and Josiah were also very young when God called them to be prophets. All of these youths called lead me to conclude that it takes the young in heart to break from certain cycles.

Jeremiah was one of the prophets the Lord spoke through to His people during the time of Daniel, Zephaniah, Ezekiel, Habakkuk, and Obadiah. Daniel, however, was the main prophet in Babylon.

Just to give you a quick perspective of time unto the birth of Christ, the order on the timeline is David, then Daniel, and then Jesus. King David (1011 BC) started to rule about 1,000 years before Christ. Then Daniel (620 BC) came into the scene about 600 years before Christ. So basically, Daniel came on the scene about 400 years after David and of course, Jesus came on the scene about 600 years after Daniel.

WHAT LED TO JERUSALEM'S CAPTIVITY?

Judah was stuck in a cycle of wickedness that eventually brought forth its captivity. It did not happen overnight. Babylon had been harassing Jerusalem for many years, but God had been begging Judah to quit their whoredom even before that. They would not listen! Several prophets, including Zephaniah and Jeremiah, warned Judah of its destruction at the beginning of King Josiah's reign. This may have had an impact on Josiah's decision for the revolution.

In Jeremiah 5:1, God told Jeremiah to search everywhere in the streets of Jerusalem to look for a man that executes judgment or seeks truth. It seems Jerusalem's condition was very similar to the condition of the times of Lot. In Genesis 19 during Lot's time, Abraham prayed so God would spare Sodom and Gomorrah if 10 people were righteous. I'm guessing Abraham figured there had to have been at least 10 righteous in the city, but obviously, there were not. Obviously 10 were not righteous but there were five that were granted permission to leave the place. In Jeremiah's time God asked for just one. How sad!

> Run ye to and fro through the streets of Jerusalem, and see
> now, and know, and seek in the broad places thereof, if ye

can find a man, if there be any that executeth judgment, that
seeketh the truth; and I will pardon it.

Jeremiah 5:1 Jeremiah received the word of the Lord and prophesied during the 13th year of the reign of King Josiah. By now, King Josiah was about 21 years old. Five years later, Josiah started a revolution from the evil the previous kings had done in the temple of God. He was a good king and reigned for 31 years. His son, Jehoikim, took the kingdom while Jeremiah was still the prophet of the time. Though the Bible does not say anything about Daniel's childhood life I trust it's safe to say that he was influenced by what was happening in Jerusalem during his upbringing.

JERUSALEM'S CAPTIVITY DURING DANIEL'S YOUTH

It is interesting to see that God was using the youth during that time. When Jeremiah tried to use the excuse that he was too young, his Creator was not shaken. God informed him that he was called even as an unformed embryo in his mother's womb.

Through all of God's beckoning to Israel through His prophets, the people would not reason with Him because they were set in their evil ways. Daniel was there as a child and developing into a young adult, watching the scene unfold. Can you imagine it for yourself?

Put yourself in Daniel's place. Looking back in my own life when I was 15 to 20 years old, I imagine this would have been a very difficult situation for me. I would probably have described it as a time of absolute chaos and confusion if another nation just came and overtook my government, my church, me, and the other people of the land. Also, I imagine the travel of 500 miles without an airplane or a car had to have been very difficult for many.

The story of Daniel is one that is extraordinary, and by extraordinary, I mean *way beyond ordinary*. It reminds me of the verse that Daniel himself wrote in the 11th chapter of his book. He writes:

And such as do wickedly against the covenant shall he corrupt by flatteries: but the people that do know their God shall be strong, and do exploits.

—Daniel 11:32

I should hope if I get in a situation like Daniel, this verse would be a reality in my life. Daniel was no average teenager. This captivity was quite a time in life for him! In fact, I cannot imagine a time in life at any age where this would have been an easy situation. Daniel, however, was extraordinary in his identity and in his God.

Captured and Chosen for Conformation

Daniel was in captivity along with all the rest of God's vessels who were in the house of God. By vessel, I mean his body. Yes, his body was one of the vessels carried out of Jerusalem into a strange land to the house of King Nebuchadnezzar. To make myself clear, let me share what the apostle Paul tells Timothy in his second letter to him. Paul makes a clear point of the value of the vessels that are in the great house, which refers to God's house. It reads:

But in a great house there are not only vessels of gold and of silver, but also of wood and of earth; and some to honour, and some to dishonour. If a man therefore purge himself from these, he shall be a vessel unto honour, sanctified, and meet for the master's use, and prepared unto every good work.

—2 Timothy 2:20–21

Daniel proved to be one of the vessels of gold and of honor, as will be proven in Chapter 2 of this writing. He was captivated and chosen to conform. Daniel was not only captured, as many others were, but he was also chosen to be conformed unto the ways of the Babylonians. He was recognized as a vessel of honor, and Babylon wanted to take advantage of his genius.

Unfortunately for them, Daniel was not willing to give his true essence to Babylon. Through his actions, Daniel said, "not happening."

CAPTURED

He was physically captured and sent to Babylon, not by his choice, but against his will, ultimately because of the sins of Judah. Daniel had to make a choice. Was he going to allow captivity of body to also result in the captivity of his soul and spirit? He decided after his capture that he was going to keep his vessel in honor. Hallelujah! He was a victim of circumstances, and he remained faithful unto God. So the story begins:

> *In the third year of the reign of Jehoiakim king of Judah came Nebuchadnezzar King of Babylon to Jerusalem and besieged it. And the Lord gave Jehoiakim King of Judah unto his hand with part of his vessels of the house of God which he carried into the land of Shinar to the house of his god and brought the vessels into the treasure house of his god.*
>
> —Daniel 1:1–2

In the very first verse of the book of Daniel, the story of the captivity of Jerusalem begins. This imprisonment was the first wave. Although there are some arguments among scholars as to the time frame, most believe the first round or wave of deportations began in 597 BC, when King Jehoiakim was also exiled with his people. King Jehoiakim was 18 years old when he began his reign, and it was in his third year of reign that Nebuchadnezzar came and took over Jerusalem.

This captivity of Daniel and his people was to last 70 years, according to the prophet Jeremiah.

> *For thus saith the Lord, That after seventy years be accomplished at Babylon I will visit you, and perform my good word toward you, in causing you to return to this place.*

—Jeremiah 29:10

CHOSEN

The king had plans for his nation and needed to choose a selection of young people to promote his agenda. Sound familiar? He specifically described wanting those of good looks, intelligence, and who were well favored. Ashpenaz, the master of the king's eunuchs, had quite a task on his hands. I'm sure he paid close attention to the king and took good notes. King Nebuchadnezzar was a very challenging man; he did not like to be disappointed. Surely Ashpenaz didn't want to be the one to upset the king—it might have cost him his head.

> *And the king spake unto Ashpenaz the master of his eunuchs, that he should bring certain of the children of Israel, and of the king's seed, and of the princes; Children in whom was no blemish, but well favoured, and skilful in all wisdom, and cunning in knowledge, and understanding science, and such as had ability in them to stand in the king's palace, and whom they might teach the learning and the tongue of the Chaldeans. And the king appointed them a daily provision of the king's meat, and of the wine which he drank: so nourishing them three years, that at the end thereof they might stand before the king.*

—Daniel 1:3–5

CONFORMATION

The word "conform" generally means "to comply with standards and rules." In Daniel's case, it was the shape and structure of Nebuchadnezzar's world or Babylonian customs. Daniel was one that was picked because he fit the request of the king to conform with a system that was different from what he knew and to mold unto Babylon's highest standards of sophistication—but Daniel had even higher standards. Daniel pledged his allegiance to the God of Israel alone. He did not want to fold to compromise.

Apostle Paul warns us not to be conformed to this world.

> *I beseech you therefore, brethren, by the mercies of God, that ye present your bodies a living sacrifice, holy, acceptable unto God, which is your reasonable service. And be not conformed to this world: but be ye transformed by the renewing of your mind, that ye may prove what is that good, and acceptable, and perfect, will of God.*
>
> —Romans 12:1–2

In the first verse, Paul tells us that the human body must be presented as a living sacrifice, which was how Daniel lived. His diet was a sacrifice. The next verse talks about the mindset not being conformed to this world. Daniel was determined to keep his mind focused by first presenting his body as a living sacrifice so that his spirit would remain connected to the Lord. He felt keeping his identity pure was very important to him.

Those chosen were chosen to conform. Yes, conformation! Yikes! Daniel was one of the youths chosen for this agenda. However, Daniel refused to conform. The word "conform" generally means "to obey rules and regulations," "to comply with rules, standards, or laws". Though

Daniel was very respectful to leadership, he had his own sets of standards. In the rest of Daniel, Chapter 1, this fact becomes very evident.

The king understood that for these young people to look like they were cosmopolitan worthy, they were to eat what he ate, drink what he drank, study what he knew, and dress like he dressed. Conforming was the plan of Babylon for Daniel. Daniel found himself in a situation where he was being groomed to look like a nation and a culture completely different from his. Yet Daniel understood that he had his own identity.

Therefore, Daniel asked Melzar, who was set over diet duty for Daniel and his three friends, to please allow him to eat his own diet instead of what the king had ordered. He reasoned with Melzar and convinced him to let him try this for 10 days. As an aside, Jesus makes an interesting statement as he speaks to the Church of Smyrna about their 10 days of tribulation in Revelation 2:10. I wonder if there's a connection. Selah moment.

This new world demanded Daniel to learn their way of speaking, to consume their diet, and to receive a name change. Daniel was okay with learning the language. He was okay with being called a different name. But he would not compromise his diet. I wonder why. Why the diet? What is so important about diet?

WHAT'S IN A DIET?

There's a saying, "You are what you eat." Each culture's diet differs from the other. What you eat affects the function of your total being: body, soul, and spirit. For example, what you eat at night can influence your dreams. Daniel took it to a greater scale. He was looking at his diet as a lifestyle. His diet was part of his identity. The Bible says that Daniel purposed in his heart that he would not eat from the king's table. He purposed in his heart. Wow! Was that pride? No, I don't think so. In fact, Daniel was very humble about it when he spoke to Melzar. It was knowledge. It was understanding. Daniel was being careful not to allow his soul to submit to that system.

There's an emotional connection with food. As a young believer, Daniel knew that. He understood that food had the ability to affect your affection or psychology. Think of how you feel when you smell the aroma of certain dishes. Daniel would not connect his heart to the Babylonian diet as the children of Israel did when they lived in Egypt. That later became burdensome for their leader Moses as he was leading them through the wilderness.

Daniel had faith in his God. He knew where his strength came from. Daniel was aware that if he ate from the king's table and became part of the masses, he would lose his identity, his anointing. He was fighting against selling his birthright, which was the relationship that he had with the God of Israel, the God who could show him dreams and the interpretation of dreams, the God who had the power to promote him in the midst of his enemies, the God who created and could lock hungry lions' mouths.

Daniel understood that he needed to be in the Spirit and not in the flesh. It was his most precious treasure. Daniel set his affection and focus on the things on high and not on the things on the earth. Therefore, when the time came, Daniel was not ashamed and had the strength to prove the perfect will of God.

And they said unto him, Thus saith Hezekiah, This day is a day of trouble, and of rebuke, and of blasphemy: for the children are come to the birth, and there is not strength to bring forth.

—Isaiah 37:3

Daniel preferred to keep his diet, the one that he knew would give him the strength to bring forth a harvest during the season that Israel needed him desperately. With the Lord's diet, Daniel had power during the day of trouble. He had a relationship, even through his diet, with the God of Israel that was higher than all the others. At the end of the 10 days of eating his own spiritual diet, Daniel was stronger and 10 times more intelligent than the rest of the students.

Church, what does your diet look like? Are you full of this world's lustful diet? What diet is fueling your intelligence? In a later chapter of this book we will talk about intelligence, especially artificial intelligence.

WHAT YOU EAT AFFECTS YOUR PROPHETIC EYE

In Daniel 2, we see that Daniel begins to benefit from setting himself apart from the rest. He and all the astrologers, the sorcerers, and the Chaldeans were in a difficult situation. This was Daniel's opportunity to prove he was God's—the One to whom he remained faithful, the God to whom he submitted his body, the One who caused his face to shine brighter than the others even while he ate a very simple diet. Daniel had not conformed.

Nebuchadnezzar dreamed dreams, wherewith his spirit was troubled, and his sleep brake from him. Then the king commanded to call the magicians, and the astrologers, and the sorcerers, and the Chaldeans, for to shew the king his dreams. So they came and stood before the king. And the king said unto them, I have dreamed a dream, and my spirit was troubled to know the dream. Then spake the Chaldeans to the king in Syriack, O king, live for ever: tell thy servants the dream, and we will shew the interpretation. The king answered and said to the Chaldeans, The thing is gone from me: if ye will not make known unto me the dream, with the interpretation thereof, ye shall be cut in pieces, and your houses shall be made a dung hill.

—Daniel 2:1–5

In this chapter of Daniel, we find that Nebuchadnezzar had a dream that he did not remember and yet insisted that the magicians and the astrologers in the land remind him of the dream and interpret it. The magicians responded that what was being requested of them was an impossible task. They told King Nebuchadnezzar that no king had ever asked for such a thing to be done. The king did not care, he simply wanted to hear the interpretation of his dream. It was something extraordinary. But Daniel lived that life that was extraordinary.

Daniel was in a very difficult situation, but he knew the God that could do the impossible. Therefore, Daniel was confident because of the sacrificial life that he lived. He was able to approach the God of Israel with faith and get the dream and its interpretation. This feat was very impressive to King Nebuchadnezzar. Daniel saved all the astrologers', the sorcerers', and the Chaldeans' lives. Nebuchadnezzar was so thrilled with Daniel's gift that he promoted Daniel and honored the God of Israel.

The book of Daniel records King Nebuchadnezzar's response to Daniel's anointing:

> *Then the king Nebuchadnezzar fell upon his face, and worshipped Daniel, and commanded that they should offer an oblation and sweet odours unto him. The king answered unto Daniel, and said, Of a truth it is, that your God is a God of gods, and a Lord of kings, and a revealer of secrets, seeing thou couldest reveal this secret. Then the king made Daniel a great man, and gave him many great gifts, and made him ruler over the whole province of Babylon, and chief of the governors over all the wise men of Babylon. Then Daniel requested of the king, and he set Shadrach, Meshach, and Abednego, over the affairs of the province of Babylon: but Daniel sat in the gate of the king.*
>
> —Daniel 2:46–49

What can we say about the king's response? Wow! If only he knew Daniel's diet. Maybe Melzar should have told the king of Daniel's secret weapon. How is it that Daniel was able to connect to the God that sees and knows all and gives interpretation of dreams? The king acknowledged Daniel's God as the God of gods, but he didn't have the strength to turn completely to this God. Sad.

WHAT'S IN A NAME?

> *Now among these were of the children of Judah, Daniel, Hananiah, Mishael, and Azariah: Unto whom the prince of the eunuchs gave names: for he gave unto Daniel the name of Belteshazzar; and to Hananiah, of Shadrach; and to Mishael, of Meshach; and to Azariah, of Abednego.*
>
> —Daniel 1:6–7

What's in a name? Why would the king change the names of the children of Israel? Names are important. You are known by your name. You are called what you are known for.

In the book of Genesis, God changed the name of Abram to Abraham in connection to Abraham's higher calling. He also changed the name of his wife from Sarai to Sarah. Each time he did this, it was because they were being called to another level.

Several other occasions in the Word of God we see name modifications, like when Jacob was changed to Israel. Did Daniel's name replacement signify a promotion in the land of the Assyrians? Yes and no! Well, maybe it was seen as a promotion to the Assyrians, but as a Jew, it was a demotion because Daniel's identity (his name) was connected to the Most High. Daniel didn't seem to fight the name change because he understood the circumstances. He understood that he was now under the leadership of King Nebuchadnezzar and that he was bound to walk in the place that he was set.

It seems the name changes were usually linked to one's assignment. In my opinion, the name changes of Daniel and his Hebrew friends were a demotion instead of a promotion. The world does that. I have a friend that used to be known by his friends in the world as Caveman. I know another that they called Sweet T. Neither of these names glorified God. Usually the names that the world gives you are a downgrading of your true identity, not an advancement toward the way God sees you.

SET APART STILL

Daniel lived a life that was set apart for Kingdom purpose even though he was grouped for the Babylonian agenda. The word of God tells us in 2 Corinthians,

> ...though we walk in the flesh, we do not war after the flesh.

> —2 Corinthians 10:3

And,

> ...for the weapons of our warfare is mighty through God...

> —2 Corinthians 10:4

Daniel displayed this truth in his life of imprisonment well. He was taken and grouped for a worldly purpose, yet he was set apart still. He would not compromise. The leaders in the government were jealous of him because there was something about Daniel that made them uncomfortable. They wanted to bring him down. A grand example of this is in the sixth chapter of Daniel where there was a conspiracy against him during the reign of King Darius.

> *It pleased Darius to set over the kingdom an hundred and twenty princes, which should be over the whole kingdom; And over these three presidents; of whom Daniel was first: that the princes might give accounts unto them, and the king should have no damage. Then this Daniel was preferred above the presidents and princes, because an excellent spirit was in him; and the king thought to set him over the whole realm. Then the presidents and princes sought to find occasion against Daniel concerning the kingdom; but they could find none occasion nor fault; forasmuch as he was faithful, neither was there any error or fault found in him. Then said these men, We shall not find any occasion against this Daniel, except we find it against him concerning the law of his God.*
>
> —Daniel 6:1–5

Daniel didn't allow being in the new land and of high status to dictate his lifestyle. He accepted the promotions and the favors from the king, but he remained faithful to his God. No matter what the status quo was, he remained set apart still. It was in this faithfulness that his God would be acknowledged as superior. This is an important premise for you and me today.

Daniel was very serious about the ways of his God. He lived with such a spirit of excellence that his enemies could not find any fault with him. They knew his discipline concerning God. They knew if they were going to trap him, it would have to be in the breaking of that discipline. They were up for a big surprise because Daniel was focused and faithful to his God.

All the presidents of the kingdom, the governors, the princes, the counselors, and the captains came together and had a meeting to conspire against the anointed one, Daniel. The story reminds me of the conspiracy against Joseph in Genesis. Remember, the Bible tells us that Joseph's brothers could not speak peaceably to him. It was utterly similar in Daniel's case. In Daniel 6:5, they called him "this Daniel," and in Daniel 6:13, they called him "that Daniel." It's almost as if they were throwing him to and fro without touching him.

In that meeting, the group of leaders produced a decree that was to last for 30 days. They took it to the king and asked him to sign and honor it. The king was not aware of the plan against Daniel, so he agreed. The decree read that if any man prayed to any other god, they were to be thrown in the lions' den. They were sure that this would work.

These presidents and governor officials laid their whole life's hope in their jobs, but Daniel was different—his hope was in his God. He was set apart still; he had not conformed to the Babylonian system. Look at Daniel's bold disposition during this conspiracy.

> *Now when Daniel knew that the writing was signed, he went into his house; and his windows being open in his chamber toward Jerusalem, he kneeled upon his knees three times a day, and prayed, and gave thanks before his God, as he did aforetime.*
>
> —Daniel 6:10

Daniel wanted to let them know that he was not intimidated. He wanted them to know his posture. In the New Testament, Apostle Paul says:

> *For me to live is Christ, and to die is gain.*
>
> —Philippians 1:21

Daniel was not going to conform to the government's way of doing things. His God was his God, and that was that. Well, of course, he was then brought to the king to be punished. But Daniel was set apart still. He was thrown in the lions' den, but even in there he was set apart still! The lions were not able to devour him.

After the king removed Daniel from the lions' den and saw the results of Daniel's relationship with God, the king made a decree to all people, nations, and languages that dwelled in all the earth and said,

> *...that in every dominion of my kingdom men tremble and fear before the God of Daniel: for he is the living God, and steadfast for ever, and his kingdom that which shall not be destroyed, and his dominion shall be even unto the end.*

—Daniel 6:26

CHAPTER TWO

THE PROPHET DANIEL'S CHARACTER

THROUGHOUT THE BOOK of Daniel, we find that Daniel had some very impressive characteristics. He was goal oriented, courteous, loyal, and respectful. He had a great attitude and persevered through tough situations. He honored those in leadership. Daniel had integrity and absolute self-control. He was also courageous, reliable, faithful, strong willed, and focused. Three of his friends, Hananiah, Mishael, and Azariah (Meshack, Shadrach, and Abednego), also had impressive strengths.

In this chapter, we're going to explore some of their ways. Before we do that, let us explore some of the characteristics of others around them, such as Nebuchadnezzar, Ashpenaz, Melzar, the magicians and astrologers, Arioch, the governmental team, Belshazzar, and the general population. We will look at the characteristics of these characters according to their contribution to the Babylonian system during Daniel's day. I believe we have these same characters today in our world as we remember

Daniel's ministry. Daniel himself is a type of "end time" character. One that was appointed by God and is used as an example of how to live in Babylon and still remain set apart unto the Lord. The book of Daniel is one of God's many ingenious ways of communicating with our generation. There are a lot of keys and clues in the book of Daniel. Those that have an ear to hear please hear what the Spirit of God is saying to the end-time church.

ASHPENAZ (MASTER OF THE EUNUCHS)

In my opinion, Ashpenaz was like the Internet. He was connected to a strong surveillance system. He was asked by the king (the Babylonian system) to bring certain ones of the children of Israel, of the king's seed, and of the princes to the king. His demeanor was cold, showing no heart or feelings, almost robotic. The revelation in this character is that of the world system is using to educate our children. This character is the device that is sent to pick and choose God's anointed or people to use them to benefit the world's system. It's a spirit. It functions as a net like the Internet during it. We must pray and watch that we are not caught in the system that demands the submitting of our essence or genius to the world's agenda.

MELZAR (SET OVER DANIEL AND THE THREE HEBREW BOYS)

These humans gathered by Ashpenaz were then handed to Melzar to be renamed, fed, and molded. Melzar's character was less robotic than Ashpenaz's. In fact, the Bible tells us that God had brought Daniel into favor with Melzar. He listened to Daniel's request to compromise his diet. He was fearful of his rulers yet had a tender heart, so he snuck in the required food for Daniel's 10-day request.

Schools and other institutions may want to be nice but have a mandate from the Babylonian system that they must conform to.

In our world today, schools and even universities and other institutions are called to change our identity to feed us so we can be molded into the world's agenda.

The Magicians and Astrologers (Power of the Gods)

Then the king commanded to call the magicians, and the astrologers, and the sorcerers, and the Chaldeans, for to shew the king his dreams. So they came and stood before the king.

—Daniel 2:2

The characteristics of the astrologers and witches of that day were fluff and powerlessness. The magicians of that time (and of all times) were limited. Daniel 2:7, 10–11, 27 prove how powerless magic is compared to one that submits to real power, the God of Israel. These witches did not have authority from the Most High God, so they had limitations. In verse 7, they told the king that they must be told the dream in order to interpret it. In verses 10–11, they told the king that no one could satisfy his request because it was a "rare thing." They said it was only the gods who do not dwell in the flesh that could answer his question. Apparently, they knew where the answer was, but they could not obtain it. Yet in verse 27, Daniel stood before the wise men, the astrologers, the magicians, the soothsayers, and the king and revealed the dream and the interpretation. They were all defeated.

Arioch (the King's Captain)

This character Arioch is hired to kill. His job was to gather all the magicians, witches, and salon, who were not able to interpret the king's dream and to kill them, period. His character was like the angel of death.

These witches, astrologers, and magicians had no idea what they were getting themselves into when they started their professions. The mercy of God challenged the assignment of death through Daniel. Daniel had the answer, and their lives were saved.

NEBUCHADNEZZAR'S INSECURITY

One of my favorite parts of Daniel's character is his humility. Daniel was not only wise but humble and gentle in his approach when dealing with the government. In comparison to Daniel's character of humility, we come face-to-face with the pride of King Nebuchadnezzar.

According to Daniel 2:1, King Nebuchadnezzar was only in the second year of the reign of his kingdom when he dreamed the dream spoken of in Daniel, second chapter. I would imagine still being pretty new at the job after only one to two years! Yet the king was a very prideful man and intended to use all his power to hide his fear and insecurity.

Daniel interpreted Nebuchadnezzar's dream, which revealed that God made him a king of kings and gave him a kingdom, power, strength, and glory. In response, the king constructed a huge statue of himself and erected it in the state of Babylon for all to worship. King Nebuchadnezzar was shaken even though he could not remember the contents of what he had dreamed. Pride, fear, and insecurity drove him to muscle, threaten, and bully his way into getting relief of his fear.

...his spirit was troubled and his sleep brake from him.

—Daniel 2:1

The king was afraid. He was so scared that he began to act irrationally. His position as a great power of the world would not allow him to humble himself and admit that he was fearful and embarrassed. Pride was his last resort. His fear, pride, and embarrassment manifested in the form of anger. He made threats to kill all the magicians. Wow! What pride. His emotions are quite unstable, going from extreme fear to extreme pride. King Nebuchadnezzar's character was indeed in question.

The king called all his magicians, astrologers, and the wise men of Babylon for help. In his fear-fueled fury, he decided unless someone reminded him of his dream and also interpreted it, he would cut all of them in pieces and turn their homes into a dump. His anger was irrational. He promised extreme harm to these innocent laborers. The truth was he just felt powerless. He was a coward.

When those brought before Nebuchadnezzar failed to tell him what he dreamed, Daniel asked Arioch, the king's captain of the guard who was sent to kill all the wise men of Babylon, what the commotion was about.

When he was told what was going on, Daniel went to the king and requested time be given to him so that he can seek God and get the interpretation. The king agreed. Next, Daniel went home and spoke with his Hebrew companions, Meshach, Shadrach, and Abednego, and convinced them to go in with him and request the mercies of the God of Heaven and inquire of Him concerning the dream and its interpretation. Daniel was obviously confident that God would give him what he asked. His heart was to save the magicians, the wise men, the Chaldeans of the land, but also his companions' lives and his own. There was no other way. King Nebuchadnezzar was like a scared, fierce animal backed up against the wall with his decree.

After time passed in the presence of God, Daniel received the interpretation in a night vision. He went to the king with confidence, told him the dream, and interpreted it.

King Nebuchadnezzar was so pleased with the interpretation of the dream that he fell on his face and worshiped Daniel even though Daniel told him that he did not have the power of interpretation but the God in heaven revealed the dream and interpretation (Daniel 2:28). The king was able to receive what he wanted from Daniel; therefore, he honored Daniel. Nebuchadnezzar chose to humble himself before men instead of

God, but God had a plan to change that. His pride would not allow him to see God as the one to be worshiped.

The king was so pleased with him that he fell on his face and worshiped Daniel and then he commanded they should offer an oblation of sweet fragrance unto Daniel. An oblation is a presentation to a god, not a human being. Of course the king was ignorant of the true and living God. He did however admit that Daniel's God was a God of gods as well as a Revealer of Secrets. Good job, king! To further honor Daniel, he promoted Daniel and made him ruler over the whole province of Babylon and chief of the governors over all the wise men of Babylon. He also honored Daniel's request to set his three friends and prayer partners, Shedrach, Meshach, and Abednego, over the affairs of the province of Babylon. What Nebuchadnezzar did next was simply boastful!

In chapter three, we find that Nebuchadnezzar felt so proud of himself because the dream interpreted his present situation as a great power. The same fear of the unknown now turned to pride after getting the knowledge. The king became boastful even as if he himself were a god. So we read in Daniel chapter 3,

> *Nebuchadnezzar made an image of gold, whose height was threescore cubits, and the breadth thereof six cubits: he set it up in the plain of Dura, in the province of Babylon.*

> —Daniel 3:1

Nebuchadnezzar actually had a golden image to be worshiped. The characteristics of King Nebuchadnezzar is that of government systems that erect those monuments that we find all over the world. These are usually placed in or on the front of government buildings. They are usually statues of kings and presidents and other figures. Those figures are actually part of Baal worship. Baal is the god of Babylon. He then sent a call to all the government officials and asked for its dedication.

Then Nebuchadnezzar the king sent to gather together the princes, the governors, and the captains, the judges, the treasurers, the counsellors, the sheriffs, and all the rulers of the provinces, to come to the dedication of the image which Nebuchadnezzar the king had set up. Then the princes, the governors, and captains, the judges, the treasurers, the counsellors, the sheriffs, and all the rulers of the provinces, were gathered together unto the dedication of the image that Nebuchadnezzar the king had set up; and they stood before the image that Nebuchadnezzar had set up.

—Daniel 3:2–3

MESHACH, SHADRACH, AND ABEDNEGO'S BOLDNESS

As the government officials were gathered around the king's statue:

Then an herald cried aloud, To you it is commanded, O people, nations, and languages, That at what time ye hear the sound of the cornet, flute, harp, sackbut, psaltery, dulcimer, and all kinds of musick, ye fall down and worship the golden image that Nebuchadnezzar the king hath set up: And whoso falleth not down and worshippeth shall the same hour be cast into the midst of a burning fiery furnace.

—Daniel 3:4–6

The mental and moral qualities distinctive to Daniel are many. His disposition is an example for all individuals in the Kingdom of God to model. The qualities of his devoted character were displayed in very difficult circumstances.

Though Daniel was indeed a great example, he was not the only one that displayed great virtue. Daniel's three companions also showed great loyalty to the God of Israel. The characteristics of Meshach, Shadrach, and Abednego is that of the Church, the body of Christ. They were confident and firm in their decision to honor God. Everyone knows about the story of Meshach, Shadrach, and Abednego. Anytime one thinks of those three, they are always associated with the fiery furnace, found in the book of Daniel, chapter 3. Let us look back and find out why these young men are associated with such a cruel image of burning.

After Daniel interpreted Nebuchadnezzar's dream in the second chapter, the king's pride led him to erect a huge statue. The third chapter of Daniel opens up with Nebuchadnezzar's ingenious idea to create this golden monument. When King Nebuchadnezzar called all of the government officials to stand before his monument, there was a mandatory call to action that the king had decreed. Anytime someone in the kingdom heard certain music, they must fall down and worship the big statue.

Here's an observation: though the king gathered all the rulers and the governors, Daniel is not mentioned among the gathering. In fact, the name of Daniel does not show up at all in the whole third chapter of the book of Daniel. In Daniel 2:48–49, we see that Daniel is promoted as ruler over the whole province of Babylon. Then Shadrach, Meshach, and Abednego were promoted over the affairs of the province. Yet the three Hebrew men are detected, but Daniel is not. Daniel for certain was in high ranks. The king called all the government officials to the dedication. Could it be because the king had already warned that no one was to pick on Daniel's God? Could it be that Daniel was their boss? Could it be that God wanted to point out the example of these three young men's character aside from Daniel?

Wow! What a command, to bow down and worship an idol! These three Hebrews could not accept that. With their hearts loyal to the God of the Hebrews, they decided to stand still. They were not going to bow down to this golden statue because they knew it was the God of all the earth that held such honor. It was Him that allowed King Nebuchadnezzar the power to overtake Israel. They were not convinced that Nebuchadnezzar nor his image was worthy of worship.

These three Jewish young men were there when the Lord God Himself revealed to Daniel the secret of the dream that caused the king to build this monument. In other words, they knew something that the king didn't know. They were wiser than the king. They understood the dream and its implications. They grew up in a society of wickedness unto the Lord and hearing the prophets prophesy Judah's doom because of Baal worship. They knew God deserved the credit. They knew the king was being foolish. They were not going to go with the flow of that foolishness. So what happened?

Daniel 3:7 says when all the people heard the music, they all fell down and worshiped. But in the next verse, it's recorded that these three Hebrews were spotted not bowing down. In Daniel 3:9–12 we find that the Chaldeans went and told the king about them breaking the decree.

THE POPULATION CURTSY TO THE WORLD'S SOUND

Then Nebuchadnezzar in his rage and fury commanded to bring Shadrach, Meshach, and Abednego. Then they brought these men before the king. Nebuchadnezzar spake and said unto them, Is it true, O Shadrach, Meshach, and Abednego, do not ye serve my gods, nor worship the golden image which I have set up? Now if ye be ready that at what time ye hear the sound of the cornet, flute, harp, sackbut, psaltery, and dulcimer, and all kinds of musick, ye fall down and worship the image which I have made; well: but if ye worship not, ye shall be cast the same hour into the midst of a burning fiery furnace; and who is that God that shall deliver you out of my hands?

—Daniel 3:13–15

After the king got the complaints, he called them in and began to question them. He gave them one last chance to worship the idol or be cast into the fiery furnace.

King Nebuchadnezzar felt he was being fair enough. The young were unflinching in their answer to the king; they were not shaken at all. The boldness that Shedrach, Meshach, and Abednego displayed was more than the king was used to.

> *Shadrach, Meshach, and Abednego, answered and said to the king, O Nebuchadnezzar, we are not careful to answer thee in this matter. If it be so, our God whom we serve is able to deliver us from the burning fiery furnace, and he will deliver us out of thine hand, O king. But if not, be it known unto thee, O king, that we will not serve thy gods, nor worship the golden image which thou hast set up.*
>
> —Daniel 3:16–18

O NEBUCHADNEZZAR, WE ARE NOT CAREFUL TO ANSWER THEE IN THIS MATTER

When they opened their mouths, they did not start by addressing him as king; they simply called him Nebuchadnezzar. I don't believe it's because they wanted to be rude to him. I believe it's because their King was the King of kings, and they wanted Nebuchadnezzar to understand that. Then the first phrase that came out of their mouths was enough for the king to immediately pronounce a death sentence on them. I believe they went in vexed and upset about the audacity of the king's edict. They were ready to fight. They were not afraid for their lives. They went in with the attitude that Esther had, "If I perish, I perish," or the attitude that we find in Revelation chapter 12:11 Which says, "And they loved not their lives unto death." This has to be, without question, the attitude of the end-time Church; otherwise, they will be conformed into the Babylonian system.

They said boldly, *"We are not careful to answer you in this matter."* The New International Version translation says, *"We do not need to defend ourselves before you in this matter."* I imagine King Nebuchadnezzar could not believe what he was hearing. How dare those three young men tell the king that they do not have to entertain him nor to defend themselves in this matter. The king was in fact a very powerful man; after all, that is why he erected the statue—it was because God had given him the power to conquer the other empires. He expected answers from those that were brought before him. The Jews took a huge chance in saying this very first phrase, but obviously they were not fearful. They were bold. They knew who the real King was. Does the church of our day know the true King? Will such boldness exist with the endtime Church?

If It Be So, Our God Whom We Serve Is Able to Deliver Us from the Burning Fiery Furnace

The next phrase that came out of their mouths was just as offensive to the king if not more so, because King Nebuchadnezzar believed he was and held all power. In a very confident posture they told the king if they are thrown into the blazing furnace, the God they serve will be able to deliver them. They informed him, one way or the other or however God decides to deliver them, they accept.

...and He Will Deliver Us out of Thine Hand, O King: But If Not, ...

This phrase showed their complete trust in God. The young men considered the possibility of God actually not delivering them. Wow! They considered it in all confidence and trust unto the Lord and were okay with that possibility. Please understand the end-time Church must consider such possibilities also and be okay with them.

In Job 13:15, Job said in his distress, *"Though he slay me, yet will I trust in him."* we must consider Philippians 1:21 in which Apostle Paul says, *"For me to live is Christ, and to die is gain."* What's amazing is that the Hebrew men were willing to be burned to death even in the face of their beloved God. They trusted God that much. They were willing to accept that type of torture even if God watched and did nothing. They did not allow fear to grip them. They looked at the worst-case scenario, and they were okay. Amazing!

...BE IT KNOWN UNTO THEE

This is actually quite a statement. It's almost as if they were saying to Nebuchadnezzar, "Know this!" They knew the God of Israel, and they wanted Nebuchadnezzar to also be aware of this knowledge. The Great God of all the earth, He is God. Know Him!

...O KING, THAT WE WILL NOT SERVE THY GODS

Wow! We will not. We will not. We will not. They boldly told the king what they absolutely will not do. They will not serve Nebuchadnezzar's gods. These young men were scholars, and they knew the Torah, the Ten Commandments.

> *Thou shalt have no other gods before me. Thou shalt not make unto thee any graven image, or any likeness of any thing that is in heaven above, or that is in the earth beneath, or that is in the water under the earth: Thou shalt not bow down thyself to them, nor serve them: for I the Lord thy God am a jealous God ....*

> —Exodus 20:2–5

...Nor Worship the Golden Image Which Thou Hast Set Up

In the declaration that the young men made to King Nebuchadnezzar, they said they would neither perform duties of service for his gods nor show adoration and reverence to the golden image. They would not serve and they would not worship. What is the difference between service and worship? To serve is to perform tasks, and to worship is to show adoration. They wanted to make it clear. They didn't want any part or type of relationship with the king's deities.

Well, of course, after such declarations, the king was left absolutely furious and called his guards to throw the three young men into the fire pit.

The Characteristics of Daniel

What have we heard about the Prophet Daniel? Let me say early on that Daniel's character is that of an end-time leader. Why is it important to know who Daniel was? Later on in this book, we'll discuss the importance of knowing Daniel's ways. We will understand the very reason why this book is written. So far, we have learned the life of Daniel, the time in life of his captivity, who he was influenced by, and we have seen a handful of personalities around him. The Bible called Daniel "the beloved" in Daniel, chapter 10, toward the end of the book. By chapter 10, it wasn't a surprise because we became quite familiar with his character by then.

Let's start from the very beginning of the story. What are some of the characteristics Daniel displayed in his book? Probably when we think about the Prophet Daniel, the first thing that comes to mind is the lions' den. Maybe for some others, it's the Daniel fast that comes to mind. Those two episodes alone were major things, while for many Bible scholars it's the end times they connect Daniel to. One of the reasons the book of Daniel is written is because I believe Daniel is a man after God's own heart for the end-time Church. He lived in the season of life similar to what we are living today. What season is that? I would call it as Daniel calls it, "The time of the end."

DANIEL'S ARRIVAL

The Prophet Daniel steps on the scene and proposes in his heart that he would not defile himself with the portion of the king's meat. As we waited to meet this chosen one, Daniel, it was evident that he would be a certain type of young man. He was described as one with no blemish, well favored, skillful in wisdom, knowledgeable, scientifically inclined, and would look like he could fit in the palace. No one imagined that he would be such a force. Daniel is one of the greatest of Bible characters in terms of virtue. His behavior showed high spiritual and moral standards. Daniel and his three friends were among the bravest of biblical figures.

In wisdom, Daniel accepted the name change. His name went from Daniel to Belteshazzar. This Babylonian name was given to him by the prince of the eunuchs. He went from a name that meant "God is my judge" to a name that meant "Who lays treasures in secret."

In defiance, he purposed in his heart that he would not defile himself with the king's dainties. In humility, he gained the favor of the very fearful prince of the eunuchs. With respect and transparency, he asked leadership for a dietary change instead of demanding his own special diet. In faith, he asked Melzar to prove him for 10 days on the diet away from the king's table. By confidence, Daniel declared to Melzar that his face would look better than the children that ate from the king's table.

The Prophet Daniel lived under an open heaven. The Bible says that Daniel and his three companions were given knowledge and skill in all learning and wisdom by God 10 times greater than the rest. Daniel was specifically gifted in understanding visions and dreams. Daniel was a winner! The king found the four young men 10 times better than all the magicians that were in all his realm. In longevity of ministry, Daniel continued even unto the first year of King Cyrus.

Daniel is famous for his fasts. Most people today take the Daniel fast lightly, but for Daniel, it was a lifestyle. He lived a very planned and systematic life. His diet, his prayer life, and fasting were all part of what made him the Prophet Daniel. There was a secret behind his gifts—it was the consecrated life that he lived. His fast cannot be duplicated as easily as some may think because there is more behind it. Fasting will always bring results, but Daniel's fast will not bring Daniel's anointing just because we copy his model. There was a high price behind such an anointing. Daniel and his three Hebrew friends were focused. There was no on and off button; they were always on. This was their lifestyle. Nebuchadnezzar's regime was not ready for such a force. Neither a lions' den nor a furnace of fire could stand before such power.

DANIEL WAS A RARE COMMODITY

He was called for by King Belshazzar's wife when she realized her husband's kingdom was in trouble. In Daniel 5, King Belshazzar put together a huge feast for thousands of his government officials and he drank wine from the Lord's vessels. God was angry, and He sent forth fingers of a man's hand and wrote on the wall. King Belshazzar was afraid of what he had seen. The king called all the magicians and astrologers, but no one could read the handwriting on the wall. The king became very fearful; his knees were knocking. Finally the queen said,

> *There is a man in thy kingdom, in whom is the spirit of the*
> *holy gods; and in the days of thy father light and understand-*
> *ing and wisdom, like the wisdom of the gods, was found in*

him; whom the king Nebuchadnezzar thy father, the king, I say, thy father, made master of the magicians, astrologers, Chaldeans, and soothsayers; Forasmuch as an excellent spirit, and knowledge, and understanding, interpreting of dreams, and shewing of hard sentences, and dissolving of doubts, were found in the same Daniel, whom the king named Belteshazzar: now let Daniel be called, and he will shew the interpretation.

—Daniel 5:11–12

The king told Daniel that he had heard of him from his father. He also told him that the magicians and the astrologers came in, but they were not able to interpret this writing on the wall. Remember, the same thing happened when Nebuchadnezzar was in power; the magicians were powerless.

King Belshazzar told Daniel that he would give him gifts and make him third ruler in the kingdom if he could tell him what the writing meant. King Belshazzar was quite foolish to think he could defile the holy vessels of God like he did. However, I admire him. Though his knees were trembling in fear of what he saw, he didn't threaten to kill anyone over the interpretation of it, as his father had done.

Daniel's purity of heart responded to the king's offer of exchanging God's precious gifts to receiving gifts and rewards of men. He told the king to keep his gifts and to give his reward to someone else. Daniel was not working for gifts. He was a gift—Daniel was priceless, and he knew it. The price that he paid for the anointing in his life was not cheap. In Daniel 9:23, the angel called him "greatly beloved." Wow! I'm sure Daniel knew his worth. After Daniel's conversation with King Belshazzar, he boldly interpreted the writing on the wall.

Daniel was highly favored.

...this Daniel was preferred above the presidents and princes, because an excellent spirit was in him; and the king thought to set him over the whole realm.

—Daniel 6:3

Daniel had an excellent spirit in him! Since his Babylonian name was Belteshazzar, which means "Who lays treasurers in secret," could it be that his fasts were laying treasures on the inside of him? How could the government in Babylon see the treasures inside of Daniel? I believe it's because of the shine in his countenance and his character traits. The spirit inside of him was shining through him. Daniel was full of treasures on the inside. Jesus, David, and hopefully you and I shine in the midst of crooked and perverse generations.

His diet was one of the sources in his treasure chest that was attributed to his spirit of excellence. He ate a diet that produced spiritual power. Remember, God attempted to feed the children of Israel manna in the wilderness as they were in their journey to the Promised Land and were subject to encountering strong enemies. Daniel ate such a type of diet. His diet honored God and kept him in connection to God.

Daniel had a defiant character, a great understanding of the times, a routine prayer life, a strict fasting life, and a wise way to respect government. He also had a remarkable gift of the prophetic. It was evident that Daniel possessed the favor of God and of man upon him. Unfortunately, that attracted jealousy and was envied by others in the world's system. Yet, because God's Word tells us that if we please Him, He will cause even our enemies to be at peace with us, Daniel prospered. Also, his prayer life caused many to buckle their knees before the lordship of his God.

Daniel's determination and consecrated life became crystal clear as his colleagues and King Darius's regime became jealous of his light and tried to overthrow him. They knew the only way they could possibly have the slightest chance of destroying him was by interfering with his conse-cration. They wanted to rob him of the secret treasures on the inside of him, but Daniel said, "No deal." They learned very quickly that Daniel was not up for negotiating with his consecration. His sanctification gave him access to the God of all gods.

Daniel had an excellent spirit from constantly chiseling away his flesh.

Besides the very famous story of the fiery furnace with the three young Jewish men, Daniel's experience in the lions' den is another that most relate to the book of Daniel. The characteristics that Daniel display here are remarkable. Very similar to his three companions, he refused to bow down to the laws of the land, which would undermine and dishonor the Lord his God. But this law was not an original law. It was a law put in place by the conspiracy of his worldly colleagues, which were jealous of his position. The colleagues tricked the king into signing this new law so they could destroy Daniel. Daniel chapter 6 starts with King Darius's promotion to Daniel, but by the fourth verse the rest of the government quickly turned against Daniel to attempt to tarnish his conduct. The conspiracy was if Daniel would not pray to the gods of Babylon, he would be thrown in the lions' den. Well, certainly he did not pray to the gods of Babylon, so he was thrown into the lions' den. Surprisingly for his colleagues, the lions were not able to devour him because God sent an angel to be with him in the lions' den. He was carrying costly treasures on the inside of him that he laid up through fasting and prayer.

DANIEL IN THE BOOK OF REVELATION

In the first six chapters of the book of Daniel, he is interpreting dreams for the government of Babylon. But from chapter 7 on, Daniel is prophesying to the generations to come. That was his main purpose. In my opinion, Daniel's life represents the lives of those living in the end times, especially leaders. I believe just as Daniel was taken into captivity, the end-time saints will find themselves in danger of the same scenario. That's my purpose for writing this book. We must be aware of Babylon, its permit for captivity, the pride in its government, its images, and the calling of the young minds for the Babylonian agenda.

The life that Daniel lived during his captivity can be an example for our generation today. Through the life of consecration that Daniel lived he received understandings of the times, which left an example for us today. We must be able to discern the times. The spirit realm was opened to him, and he had access to revelations that he desperately needed. When he needed access and revelation of the king's dream God gave them to him. When Daniel needed protection from the lions, he was safe. When he needed intelligence after 10 days of eating pulse instead of the king's diet, he had it above and beyond the others'.

I also find that the book of Revelation and the book of Daniel are quite in tune with each other. In the book of Revelation, it seems that the generation will be in very tough times and will need access to the supernatural realm even as Daniel did.

In research for one of my teachings called, "Dancing for the End Time Harvest in the Nations," about 10 years ago, I came to realize how closely related the book of Daniel and the book of Revelation were. One interesting fact that I discovered was the angel in both books instructed their writer, Daniel and John, concerning their prophetic timing.

I have always had an interest in the end times, but this discovery took my interest to another level. These two books of the Bible are very closely related. In the last chapter of both books the angel that's speaking to the writer commands the timing of the writing perspective. The command dictated the appropriate time or season for the reading of their writing. This was the only time this happened in the Bible. I believe this is a big clue to those that want to pay attention to the generation of the end times.

Daniel 12:4 reads, "But thou Daniel, shut up the words, and seal the book, even to the time of the end." Revelation 22:10 reads, "And he said unto me, Seal not the saying of the prophecy of this book: for the time is at hand." Both angels tell their writers the appropriate timing of what they were seeing. I would think the end time generation may want to pay attention to the man Daniel because his character merited him to see the things of the end-time generation. Daniel's life was prophetic of the timing of his message.

Chapters 7–12 of the book of Daniel hold keys of events for our lives today. In the next chapter of this writing, we are going to look at Daniel's influence, not only in Babylon, but also in our generation and generations to come.

CHAPTER THREE

THE PROPHET DANIEL'S INFLUENCE

THEN GOD CREATED Adam and Eve, He told them to subdue and to have dominion. Influence! This man Daniel seemed to have done just that with everyone that he came in contact with. Daniel was in captivity yet had dominion. How was that possible? God helped him, or more specifically, through a relationship with God, Daniel influenced many. Let me say not all relationships are created equally. Some have closer and deeper relationship with God than others. Daniel was one that had a very close relationship with God.

> *For many are called, but few are chosen.*
>
> —Matthew 22:14

Even in the case of Daniel and his friends, there was evidence that some were closer to God than others. All four were taken into captivity.

All four were picked for the king's care and agenda. All four were great believers. But only Daniel stood out as he did. Why? I don't know. What we do know is that Daniel was chosen by God to stand out. What we also know is that we can be influenced by him now just as many others were during his lifetime.

What was his secret? Well, we can look at his source and his total reliance upon that source. When we submit ourselves under the mighty hand of God, which was Daniel's source, He becomes our treasure, our secret weapon. That's what Daniel did—he made God his priceless treasure.

DANIEL INFLUENCED HIMSELF

Daniel influenced himself. How did Daniel influence himself? Daniel was able to possess his own soul. He proved what Jesus instructs us in Luke 21:19. Through his prayer life and his disciplined diet, Daniel was empowered with self-discipline. We must not underestimate the power of such disciplines as fasting and prayer. They are invisible sources behind a victorious and successful life. Jesus tells us:

In your patience possess ye your souls...

—John 21:19

Daniel must have had a lot of patience. He was full of self-control. He didn't allow position to control his identity in God. He was not moved by gifts. He influenced his own soul. He kept his emotions in check. He prayed three times a day, and it was through prayer that he received answers from God.

Daniel was disciplined, and he lived a fasted life. He was able to fast for 21 days without fear, a type of fast that has revolutionized many Christians' lives. Daniel had to purpose in his heart not only for his diet but for many other decisions that had to be made in his life. This type of focus and determination allotted him the ladder up to the throne of God. He influenced himself to have a relationship with the Most High God.

DANIEL INFLUENCED HIS COMPANIONS

How did Daniel influence Meshach, Shadrach, and Abednego? We know they all went into captivity at the same time as Daniel. They all fit the description that Ashpenaz was given that the king was looking for. We also know they were all four called into the Babylonian government for a common purpose. Is that how they met each other? The book of Daniel does not tell us.

It seems Daniel stood higher than the other three. Daniel was the spokesman for the four of them. The Bible does not tell us their living arrangements except to say that Daniel went home and made the news known to the other three young men about the king's extreme decree. They all came together in prayer and consecration to hear from God about King Nebuchadnezzar's dream.

By looking at these relationships, I am sure they influenced one another in some ways. However, Daniel being the main prophet of the land during this time in Babylon, I imagine he had more influence over the three than they had over him.

What we know for sure is that Daniel was the brightest light bulb in the group because on every occasion he was set apart. He was called to the frontline for all the interpretations. That tells us that his gift was stronger than the others'.

Then said Daniel to Melzer, whom the prince of the eunuchs had set over Daniel, Hananiah, Mishael, and Azariah, Prove thy servants, I beseech thee, ten days; and let them give us pulse to eat, and water to drink. Then let our countenances

be looked upon before thee, and the countenance of the chil-
dren that eat of the portion of the king's meat: and as thou
seest, deal with thy servants.

—Daniel 1:11–13

From the very first chapter our attention is pulled to Daniel's influence over his friends. When he spoke to Melzar concerning the meal arrangements, Daniel did not speak only of himself; instead he used the word "us." Daniel was an advocate not only for himself but also for his three companions. They obviously had become friends and had a good understanding of how they wanted to live in captivity. Daniel influenced the diet of his three friends. He somewhat went in as a type of intercession for them as he negotiated their meal plan. He was the middle man between his three companions and Melzar.

In Daniel, chapter 2, the Bible tells us that God gave Daniel the interpretation of the dream. Although Daniel involved his friends in the time of consecration, God made the secret known to Daniel. I would imagine once Daniel received the interpretation, his friends' faiths were built. Influenced! To see the possibility that they could influence the lives of so many must have built their faith as well. Remember, if the king didn't receive the dream and its interpretation, he was ready to kill all the magicians, the astrologers, the Chaldeans, and even Daniel and his friends, according to Daniel 2:13.

Their friend Daniel convinced them to go to God by faith, and all these lives were spared. How do you think they felt about Daniel from this experience? How would you have felt? I'm sure I would have thanked Daniel for the opportunity to be a part of this amazing time in history.

Then Daniel went to his house, and made the thing known
to Hananiah, Mishael, and Azariah, his companions: That
they would desire mercies of the God of heaven concerning

this secret; that Daniel and his fellows should not perish with
the rest of the wise men of Babylon.

—Daniel 2:17–18

Daniel chapter two notes another account of Daniel's influence on behalf of his friends. Daniel was a man of integrity, a faithful and honorable friend. After his friends came alongside him in prayer and fasting for the answer of the dream and its interpretation, he didn't forget them. When the king decided to reward him, he requested the promotion of his friends as well. Because of Daniel's integrity, his companions were influenced by receiving job positions of higher status and pay. He was constantly pulling them up higher.

Then the king made Daniel a great man, and gave him many
great gifts, and made him ruler over the whole province of
Babylon, and chief of the governors over all the wise men of
Babylon. **Then Daniel requested of the king,** *and he set*
Shadrach, Meshach, and Abednego, over the affairs of the
province of Babylon: but Daniel sat in the gate of the king.

—Daniel 2:48–49 (emphasis mine)

DANIEL INFLUENCED ASHPENAZ

Ashpenaz, as master of Nebuchadnezzar's eunuchs, was given the strictest criteria that the king required of the Israelite young subjects. He was to select and to bring certain children of specific standards before the king for training of the king's service.

Ashpenaz was given a list of qualifications, which Daniel obviously met. I think it's safe to say that Daniel made an impression on the king's eunuch when he laid eyes on him and saw his "resume." Therefore, Ashpenaz chose him as one of the Israelites to be groomed because he was impressed by him.

The prince of the eunuchs gave the new subjects Babylonian names. Daniel was given the name of Belteshazzar, which means "Who lays up treasures in secret." I believe when the prince saw Daniel, he was able to see deeper than meets the eye. Daniel carried the God that reveals secrets in the inside of him, and those appointed over him sensed it. In Daniel's story it is obvious that God brought Daniel into favor and tender love with others.

DANIEL INFLUENCED MELZAR

Melzar, the prince of the eunuchs, was not only afraid of losing his job but his very life. His job was to care for the lab rats, I mean the young scholars the king had called for. This was the king's big project. He took it very seriously because he knew it was the future of his kingdom. He had an exact formula for their grooming.

> *And the king appointed a daily provision of the king's meat, and of the wine which he drank.*
>
> —Daniel 1:5

He would not have taken too kindly to Melzar messing with his projects.

Certainly the king was not familiar with this diet that Daniel was proposing. The king wanted them to eat his portion because he believed that's what was going to bring him the results he was looking for. But Daniel had his own diet. Daniel had not proven the king's dainties to bring wholeness.

There were others in the Bible that had their own way, which deferred from the world's system. David, for instance, would not allow King Saul to give his physical armor. He had secrets about battle that

King Saul had no knowledge of. David's strength relied on the strategies of God.

> *David said unto Saul, I cannot go with these; for I have not proved them. And David put them off him.*
>
> —1 Samuel 17:39

Nebuchadnezzar was raising what he felt were government giants. That's a very serious matter. Yet, Melzar compromised because Daniel had his attention. Daniel 1:9 tells us that God Himself had brought Daniel into "favor and tender love" with Melzar. Melzar didn't have a chance. God himself had touched his heart concerning Daniel. He made a deal with Daniel because God had stepped into the situation. Influence!

The diet that Daniel proposed for his three scholarly friends and himself didn't seem very appealing. It was just pulse, which is basically beans and seeds for food and only water for drink. He initially proposed this diet for 10 days and Melzar agreed because he liked Daniel. He was also influenced at the end of the 10 days when he saw the miracle of Daniel's diet.

DANIEL INFLUENCED ARIOCH

When no one was found that could remind the king of his dream, much less interpret it, Arioch was sent by decree to kill all the wise men of the land, which included Daniel and his three friends (Daniel 2:7–15). Daniel pulled Arioch aside and said something that changed Arioch's heart. Influence!

> *Then Daniel answered with counsel and wisdom to Arioch the captain of the king's guard, which was gone forth to slay the wise men of Babylon:*
>
> —Daniel 2:14

Daniel's conversation with a ruthless guard was so wise and gentle that he changed his assignment. Arioch's job was to kill, but instead he arranged a meeting between the king and Daniel. Wow!

Daniel went to the king and requested time from the king. Daniel asked Arioch for time with the king. Then Daniel asked the king for time with the King of the kings. His plan was to go into intercession unto the King for the king. Daniel knew God is the true King that reveals secrets. That was his sure plan to get the dream and its interpretation. After time had passed, Daniel went before the king and interpreted the dream. Certainly, Arioch was relieved that he did not have to gather all these men to be killed. Arioch was influenced by Daniel.

DANIEL INFLUENCED THE MAGICIANS, ASTROLOGERS, SORCERERS, AND CHALDEANS

Daniel not only influenced individuals but also groups of people. Several times the magicians, astrologers, sorcerers, and Chaldeans came before the kings to interpret dreams, but they were not able to get nor give the interpretations. Most of those times, the interpretations were in the fist of God. Daniel, however, was able to open the hand of God and release the secrets of these visions. The wise men of the land sat back and watched this young man run circles around them. Also, at the end of Daniel 2, the magicians and other evil powers of the land were present when the king himself worshiped Daniel and lifted up the name of His God. They were all influenced by Daniel's influence on the king.

DANIEL'S INFLUENCE ON KINGS

Daniel lived through the reigns of King Nebuchadnezzar, King Belshazzar, King Darius, and King Cyrus. In this book, we will take notice that Daniel's anointing encounters not only kings of his day but also future kings and presidents of our nations today and in the future.

God left his example of Daniel's life for you and me in this generation and generations to come. As we learn of his character and influence, we also will know how to live in such times and have such influence with our government. Daniel was not afraid of the kings. He influenced the kings. Daniel brought the kings down to their knees before the God that he served. They favored Daniel. They called upon Daniel for guidance and even leadership. Daniel really had a way with kings. He was very confident in his God, who is the ultimate King. He was impressive with ease. His charm was the anointing of God. In the book of Daniel, with the exception of chapter 3, Daniel dealt with kings from chapter 1 all the way through chapter 6. Why so much? Daniel was always being called on by leadership for something. Daniel received several promotions and gifts. It's interesting that in just about every case, the kings would bow down and honor the God of Daniel. Unfortunately, there were times they would even worship Daniel in the same way.

Daniel was so honored by the king that he was able to ask King Nebuchadnezzar to set Shadrach, Meshach, and Abednego over the affairs of the province of Babylon. Daniel was so highly influential in Nebuchadnezzar's life that he passed Daniel's reputation along to generations of kings after him.

When Belshazzar was troubled about the writing on the wall, the queen called for Daniel. Immediately Belshazzar remembered Daniel's reputation from his father and rehearsed it to Daniel. King Darius was just as impressed. In fact, King Darius was very extremely fond of Daniel.

When Daniel stood before Nebuchadnezzar the king said,

As for these four children, God gave them knowledge and skill
in all learning and wisdom: and Daniel had understanding
in all visions and dreams.

—Daniel 1:17

And the king communed with them; and among them all was found none like Daniel, Hananiah, Mishael, and Azariah: therefore stood they before the king. And in all matters of wisdom and understanding, that the king enquired of them, he found them ten times better than all the magicians and astrologers that were in all his realm.

—Daniel 1:19–20

Daniel and the Hebrew young men were already 10 times better than all the magicians and astrologers that were in all the king's realm, and most of magicians and astrologers practiced their craft for many years or most of their lives. Daniel 1:17 tells us that it's God who gave these men the skills they needed to become so influential to the king.

There's great evidence of Daniel's influence upon the king at the end of Daniel, chapter 2.

Then the king Nebuchadnezzar fell upon his face, and worshipped Daniel, and commanded that they should offer an oblation and sweet odours unto him. The king answered unto Daniel, and said, Of a truth it is, that your God is a God of gods, and a Lord of kings, and a revealer of secrets, seeing thou couldest reveal this secret.

—Daniel 2:46–47

Nebuchadnezzar worshiped Daniel; an extreme thing for a king to do. Then he admits that Daniel's God is bigger than the Babylonian god. King Nebuchadnezzar was truly impressed and influenced by Daniel and his God.

In Daniel 4, King Nebuchadnezzar had another dream that needed interpretation, so he sent for Daniel again. This time, it was a very sad situation for the king, but at least this time he admitted that he was fearful of that first dream. Daniel was able to calm King Nebuchadnezzar since he was confident in Daniel's gift. Look at how he addressed Daniel in this chapter:

> *O Belteshazzar, master of the magicians, because I know that the spirit of the holy gods is in thee, and no secret troubleth thee, tell me the visions of my dream that I have seen, and the interpretation thereof.*
>
> —Daniel 4:9

In Daniel 4:9 the king called him master, master of the magicians. How impressive!

The king seemed troubled and afraid of some of these dreams that he did not understand because they were out of his control, but Daniel had the answer. He trusted Daniel's gift. After Daniel interpreted the dream, he attempted to counsel the king to go a different direction. Daniel's tender heart was broken by what was due to happen to the king because of his pride. Unfortunately, the king was not influenced by Daniel's counsel. The king's pride was influencing him and caused him to dismiss Daniel's advice. But by the end of this chapter, we find that he was influenced by God's judgment upon his pride.

> *Now I Nebuchadnezzar praise and extol and honour the King of heaven, all whose works are truth, and his ways judgment: and those that walk in pride he is able to abase.*
>
> —Daniel 4:37

DANIEL INFLUENCED KING BELSHAZZAR AND HIS WIFE

The next king who stepped on the scene was Belshazzar, who succeeded his father Nebuchadnezzar. King Belshazzar decided to have a big party for about a thousand people. He got drunk and was influenced to bring the gold and silver goblets out of his dad's house to serve wine to his guests in. Maybe he wasn't aware, but those vessels were taken out of the temple of God in Jerusalem and were holy. But since he was drunk, I'm not sure that would make a difference to him even if he knew.

> *They drank wine, and praised the gods of gold, and of silver, of brass, of iron, of wood, and of stone.*

> —Daniel 5:4

Oh no, what a ritual! This ritual was as the one that happened at the bottom of the mountain with the children of Israel when Moses went up to get the Commandments from God. During the exodus, the children of Israel took off their jewelry, melted them, and had a party, worshiping the golden calf that they manufactured with the gold that God himself had provided them. What a slap in God's face in both cases.

King Belshazzar was enjoying the festive occasion with his guests without fear of God and without regard for God's feeling for using his holy vessels. Then something very scary happened. The king saw fingers writing on the wall of the palace out of thin air. He didn't know what to do and was very afraid. He was literally shaking in his boots. Of course he ran to magic for the answer. He called for all of the magicians, astrologers, and soothsayers even as his father used to do and offered them all kinds of gifts and positions in the government if they could interpret what was written, but no answer came.

What happened next proved how influential Daniel really was in Babylon. The king's wife, who obviously was influenced by Daniel, knew he was the only answer. She reminded her husband of what happened when his father, Nebuchadnezzar, was king.

> *Now the queen by reason of the words of the king and his lords came into the banquet house: and the queen spake and said, O king, live for ever: let not thy thoughts trouble thee, nor let thy countenance be changed: There is a man in thy kingdom, in whom is the spirit of the holy gods; and in the days of thy father light and understanding and wisdom, like the wisdom of the gods, was found in him; whom the king Nebuchadnezzar thy father, the king, I say, thy father, made master of the magicians, astrologers, Chaldeans, and soothsayers; Forasmuch as an excellent spirit, and knowledge, and understanding, interpreting of dreams, and shewing of hard sentences, and dissolving of doubts, were found in the same Daniel, whom the king named Belteshazzar: now let Daniel be called, and he will shew the interpretation.*
>
> —Daniel 5:10–12

She began by letting the king know that there was already a man in his kingdom with the knowledge to help him. I'm sorry to say, but it's almost as if the king were clueless. He did not know his father's activities, and he did not know of Daniel's work; it took the queen to point it out to him. Perhaps the king was an alcoholic or was just a spoiled kid who didn't pay attention and was not prepared for his job. How was it possible that he didn't know about Daniel?

But wait, were the other magicians and astrologers not aware of Daniel either? How can that be? They were deeply influenced by his work before in times past. These magicians and astrologers were aware that their lives and the lives of their colleagues was spared during the days of King Nebuchadnezzar. They must have remembered the times when Daniel was the only one that could interpret.

Even though the king didn't know about Daniel, in Daniel 5:10–12 we find that the queen was very influenced by Daniel's work. She remembered his work in king Nebuchadnezzar's kingdom. She made her way into the banquet house to go talk to her husband about Daniel because her husband was afraid. The king sent for Daniel, and Daniel boldly interpreted the vision. By the end of the interpretation, King Belshazzar knew Daniel had the correct interpretation. He commanded that Daniel be clothed with scarlet and a gold chain be placed around his neck, and he also promoted him to third ruler.

Unfortunately, Belshazzar's life was taken from him that very night. He was quite influenced by Daniel's work as he took his last breaths.

DANIEL INFLUENCED KING DARIUS

Now King Darius of Persia was in his early 30s when he took the kingdom from Belshazzar. Daniel chapter 6 starts by telling us King Darius's setup for his government. Daniel was at the top of his list for placement.

> It pleased Darius to set over the kingdom an hundred and twenty princes, which should be over the whole kingdom; And over these three presidents; of whom Daniel was first: that the princes might give accounts unto them, and the king should have no damage. Then this Daniel was preferred above the presidents and princes, because an excellent spirit was in him; and the king thought to set him over the whole realm.
>
> —Daniel 6:1–3

Obviously, Daniel's influence upon the Persian king was grand. What was it about Daniel? King Darius just took over, and these were his actions toward Daniel as he set up his ruling system. The king had such a heart for the prophet. What divine favor Daniel had, but, of course, it came with a price.

The members of the government tried to overthrow him because they were jealous of him. They conspired together to destroy him. They put in place a royal statute for the king to sign, which they hoped would get rid of Daniel. The statute said, "Whosoever shall ask a petition of any God or man for thirty days except unto the king should be cast into the lions' den." This was indeed a trap, but Daniel was not influenced by them. Therefore, Daniel made petitions to his God as he had always done without regard to the statute. Then they brought Daniel as accused before the king, and Daniel was thrown into the lions' den. King Darius was deeply concerned because his heart was with Daniel. The evil plan bound the king to the constitution of the land. King Darius was in distress for Daniel, but he had to follow the law of the land that he himself had signed.

> *Then the king went to his palace, and passed the night fasting: neither were instruments of musick brought before him: and his sleep went from him. Then the king arose very early in the morning, and went in haste unto the den of lions. And when he came to the den, he cried with a lamentable voice unto Daniel: and the king spake and said to Daniel, O Daniel, servant of the living God, is thy God, whom thou servest continually, able to deliver thee from the lions?*
>
> —Daniel 6:18–20

What happened next is amazing and really shows the heart of the king toward Daniel. He was angry with Daniel's evil accusers, and he wanted them to pay. He demanded that the men who accused Daniel be brought in and thrown in the lions' den themselves, along with their children and their wives. Then Darius made a decree that in every dominion of his kingdom, men should tremble before the God of Daniel. Wow! Once again Daniel influenced another king.

DANIEL INFLUENCED GOD

Did Daniel influence God? Yes! Can a man influence God? Sure! That's the purpose of prayer and fasting. In Jeremiah chapter 9, even during the time that Daniel was living, God said to call for the wailing women, that they may take up a wail to appease His fury. God was weary of the wickedness and whoredom of His people. They were operating in opposition to God's laws. At that time, the children of Israel's sins were extremely intense.

Can God be influenced by our intercession? Absolutely, and we see this happen with Moses as he stood in the gap for Miriam. Time after time, intercession has influenced God. God is influenced by His beloved people. This is on both sides of the spectrum: good or bad. The children of Israel have been known to bring God to a place of fury many times, but He is absolutely able to be influenced positively, or shall I say impressed, by a man's way of living.

And he said unto me, O Daniel, a man greatly beloved....

—Daniel 10:11

Daniel melted the heart of God. When Daniel was on his knees, he activated the heavens, and an angel was sent to bring Daniel the message that he was in petition of. Daniel moved the heavens! God was moved by the life that Daniel lived, and He was pleased. Daniel shook heaven and earth. His passion for God made kings bow. His consecration confronted cultures. His sanctification starved gods of the underworld. His appetite set him apart from the world unto the Lord.

Daniel was one of those men. He touched God in the deepest way. He honored God as God. He caused Kings to bow down their knees to God. He lived a life that allowed the anointing of God to flow through him so well that the magicians of the land were not able to compete.

Daniel Influenced Generations after Him

We have looked at a lot of people that Daniel influenced in the actual book of Daniel. However, Daniel's greatest influence has been on the generations that came after him. In fact, in the last verse of the book of Daniel the angel informs him that he will be laying in his grave at the time of the end. The angel meant that Daniel would be long dead. This was to inform Daniel that his visions were for generations to come. Daniel was simply chosen to be revealed of those things but would not live to see them himself. His life was used as a message for generations that would come after him.

Has Daniel influenced you yet? I am definitely influenced by this prophet. He was given revelation of all the governmental systems of this world, from the captivity of Jerusalem to all governments' final fall even to the end of all things. Don't overlook this because it will help you to understand how Daniel is to influence you. It will also help you to understand the importance of his influence on your life.

We find that in the last seven chapters of Daniel, he began to receive revelation from God concerning the end times.

That certainly includes you and me. Keep in mind that revelation was being given to him from the day of their captivity according to Nebuchadnezzar's dream. The influence of the book of Daniel spans as far forward as the end of the days. Daniel is an end-time prophet. He is prophesying to you and I today.

Look at the last six words from the book of Daniel.

...at the end of the days.

—Daniel 12:13

It does not say the end of "his" days even though the angel is talking directly to him. It says the end of "the" days, which signifies the end times.

But go thou thy way till the end be: for thou shalt rest, and stand in thy lot at the end of the days.

—Daniel 12:13

Daniel had to have such influence over all the kings, their visions, their plans, and their wisdom because his influence was just that timely. The book of Daniel shows the sovereignty plan of God for humanity, especially for God's remnant, you and I. The book of Daniel is a prophetic book. It is evident that Daniel is an end-time prophet. The book of Daniel seems to take us from the captivity of God's people to the end of the days even to the second coming of Christ. Daniel 12:2 is the rapture of the Church or the second coming of Christ, however you choose to see it. There are several clues to help us see the time span of Daniel's prophetic life.

Throughout this book we have already discussed several of these clues and will continue to discuss more of them. One obvious indictor that Daniel is positioned to influence our generation is found in the connection of its brother book, the book of Revelation, as we briefly discussed earlier.

The end-time Church needs to be able to spiritually stand before the government system of the kingdoms of this world with no blemish, well favored, skillful, in all wisdom and knowledge and royalty. Yet we must not allow ourselves to be completely overtaken and used by this world's system. Therefore, Daniel's life is an important model for us. Daniel as a prophet represents us as the people of God. I hope you are influenced because I believe we must be able to model his life that we may be victorious over the devices of the enemy in the end times.

But thou, O Daniel, shut up the words, and seal the book,
even to the time of the end: many shall run to and fro, and
knowledge shall be increased.

—Daniel 12:4

This is one of the most impressive verses to me from the prophet Daniel. What really stands out is that this verse from the last chapter of the book of Daniel is tied to a verse in the last chapter of the book of Revelation.

And he saith unto me, Seal not the sayings of the prophecy of
this book: for the time is at hand.

—Revelation 22:10

Wow! On these two circumstances, these words are spoken by a heavenly host. The angel that was talking to Daniel gave him a command, and the angel that was speaking to John gave him a command. It is almost as if the angel that was talking to John came on assignment to continue the work of the angel that was talking to Daniel. Was it the same angel?

CHAPTER FOUR

ARE WE IN CAPTIVITY?

And they said unto him, Thus saith Hezekiah, This day is a day of trouble, and of rebuke, and of blasphemy: for the children are come to the birth, and there is not strength to bring forth.

—Isaiah 37:3

I START THIS chapter with this particular verse because of its emphasis on time and on strength. It refers to time as "this day." It tells what type of time it is. It names "this day" as trouble, rebuke, and blasphemous, and then it tells us why. The verse says that God's people were weak, and they didn't have the power needed to bring forth what was at hand to bring forth. As I wrote this chapter, I felt that this verse was quite appropriate to start with. This is in comparison to the days of the captivity of Jerusalem, this day which king Hezekiah is speaking of, and the times that we are living in today. What time is it?

What Time Is It?

But thou, O Daniel, shut up the words, and seal the book, even to the time of the end....

—Daniel 12:4a

...for the time is at hand.

—Revelation 22:10b

Have you taken a moment in the past few months or weeks to ponder about what time it is on God's prophetic time clock? God, in his infinite wisdom, always takes time into consideration. Time is very significant. I think it is time that we take the time to think about what "time" it really is.

As we study the book of Daniel, we've come to see that the very first thing that is pointed out is time.

In the third year of the reign of Jehoiakim king of Judah came Nebuchadnezzar king of Babylon unto Jerusalem, and besieged it.

—Daniel 1:1

This verse tells us the when, the who, the where, and what happened. Now let's look at the time of Jerusalem's captivity.

When?

In the third year of the reign of Jehoiakim...

—Daniel 1:1a

It was a set time for Jerusalem to be besieged. It wasn't because that's what God wanted, it was because their evil activities had brought them to the fullness of time. God cautioned them repeatedly, but they would not take heed of His warnings. God is slow to anger, but he calculates His timing to release punishment and discipline in due time.

God is gracious, and His judgment is calculated and appointed. Hebrews 9:27 says, *"Even as it is appointed unto man once to die then comes judgment."* That verse is about man's judgment, and it also speaks of timing. I think it's fair to say that we should take time into greater consideration. As you read this book. I would like to open your heart and your mind so you're able to see the Kingdom of God as it truly is in its timing.

As we enter the time in the end times, what did Jesus have to say in his teachings? Jesus said in Matthews 24 that the last days would be as in the days of Noah. What was He saying? He was referring to the activities going on in the earth, but He was also pointing out the time. The timing of Noah was one that brought God to release wrath on mankind, just as the timing of Daniel was a time that brought God's wrath upon Jerusalem.

Look around and see if you can see evidence of this. Apostle Paul describes the last days as "perilous times." What did he say would make the time perilous? The activities that will take place. Look around you and see if times are indeed perilous. In fact, look at the activities that he prophesied in the last days. Do you see those activities this day? It's the times. When Paul said, "This know" he meant, be aware of this or have knowledge of this.

This know also, that in the last days perilous times shall come.
For men shall be lovers of their own selves, covetous, boasters,
proud, blasphemers, disobedient to parents, unthankful,
unholy, Without natural affection, trucebreakers, false
accusers, incontinent, fierce, despisers of those that are good,

Traitors, heady, highminded, lovers of pleasures more than lovers of God; Having a form of godliness, but denying the power thereof: from such turn away.

—Timothy 3:1–3

If you are reading this book, I choose to believe that you have eyes to see and ears to hear. If you do not, I pray that the Lord opens your eyes to see and your ears to hear what the Spirit of God is saying. We are living in perilous times—times of the end and approaching a time of captivity. Some have already been captured.

Some years ago, I believe it was 2012, I felt that the Holy Spirit was saying to me that we are in a season now that the enemy is going to begin to try to overtake our bodies into captivity. The battle was going to become stronger than ever before. In other words, he would try to invade our actual vessels.

What I was sensing at the time were plans that were already at play, but we were not yet aware of them. Later, we would come to see it more plainly. By 2020, this captivity was evident. Today we see it quite plainly. And from now on, it will become more and more so until the day of our redemption by our Savior Jesus Christ.

Also, I had a vision around 2015 of a person sitting in front of a device like a computer, and they were typing. Their fingers were becoming almost the same material as the keyboard, and they were transforming into an electronic device. As they continued to type, the transformation was moving toward their arms to finally consume that person's whole being. The person was becoming one with the computer. At the time of the vision, I did not understand it. Today, I can say I do. Overtaken! Captivity!

THE NEBUCHADNEZZAR OF TODAY

Jesus says,

The thief cometh not, but for to steal, and to kill, and to destroy…

—John 10:10

Who is the thief? The thief is the tempter. When Satan comes, he comes to kill us, to steal from us, and to destroy us. He always has an agenda, and it's never to our benefit. Once we are enticed and we decide to compromise, we are captured.

But every man is tempted, when he is drawn away of his own lust, and enticed.

—James 1:14

THE ASHPENAZ OF TODAY

And he causeth all, both small and great, rich and poor, free and bond, to receive a mark in their right hand, or in their foreheads: And that no man might buy or sell, save he that had the mark, or the name of the beast, or the number of his name.

—Revelation 13:16–17

THE NET IS A WEB

The Internet is exactly what it says it is—a net. It's a web that catches us in it, and we become part of it. Like a spider, the devil builds a web and awaits its prey to walk in and be captured. Do insects not know that the spiderweb is going to catch them and they will be consumed by the spider? The way to understand this concept is to remember First Peter 5:8 as it reads, "…the devil as a roaring lion goeth about, seeking whom he may devour." I find it interesting how the name of this system is exactly what it's built for, and yet we still walk right in. The very language of the Internet or websites tell us what we're walking into, so how can we not know? Help us, Lord!

Most of us know the language of some of these danger zones. For example: my cell phone is a Galaxy (that's the name of the model). Apple's logo is a bitten fruit. Starbucks' logo is a woman with powers of heavens, seas, and earth, which reminds me of the woman in the book of Revelation. What in the world is wrong with us? Are these logos and names of these devices and products not telling us clearly enough? We also get commands to ask for our agreement as we download things and surf sites on the web. We are asked to allow or to block. Allow is like saying "amen," which means "I agree." Most of the times they are asking you to allow them to connect you and all your identity to other systems. The net or web at its best! It also likes to know our location, and we give it! Sometimes they even ask to tell them if you're a robot or not. What is that about?

When they ask our permission for all of this, we're likely to just give it up because we want what we want—the information they've got. Self-control is a big problem in our generation.

There are countless statistics these days about people and their devices. We found many years ago that people with keyboard jobs can develop this condition called carpal tunnel syndrome, which can cause numbness of the hands. We also know that children and adults become addicted to their devices. In fact, if you go to a salon and look around, you will find that everyone has a phone on their hands. They are checking either their text messages, emails, Facebook, WhatsApp, or just looking and browsing other apps or the web. We have become deeply connected to the Internet.

Keep your identity; remember who you are.

There's a reason this book is called *Remember Daniel* and the subtitle is *And don't forget the days of Noah*. It is crucial that we are sure in our identity to be able to stand strong in the days that we are living in right now. Otherwise, we will be consumed and overtaken.

There is a strong connection between the book of Daniel and the book of Revelation. "Revelation" means "the unveiling." So the angel tells John to open the books. Are you ready for your eyes to be opened?

In the last chapter of Daniel, the angel tells Daniel to close the book because it's not yet time. Yet in the book of Revelation in the very last chapter, the angel tells John the Revelator to open the book because the time is at hand. In both accounts we are led to understand that there will be knowledge revealed to us in the last days.

The angel tells Daniel that knowledge will become great. We must live as Daniel lived so that we can get revelation in this hour. Let me say that again. We must live as Daniel lived so that we can get revelation in this hour. The times are perilous. Daniel 12:4 is where the angel tells Daniel the prophet to shut the books. It is also the exact same verse that he says knowledge shall be increased. How? How will knowledge be increased? Well, to know how knowledge will be increased we'd have to open our ears to hear what the angel told John the revelator at Patmos.

And he saith unto me, Seal not the sayings of the prophecy of this book: for the time is at hand.

—Revelation 22:10

In essence, the angel in Daniel is saying, once they hear it, then they'll understand. It's in the last days that we come to know and understand what Daniel had to seal.

John was encouraged to open the books because of the appointed time. Knowledge! The time is now. We must be sober and vigilant. Also keep in mind that Daniel is in fact talking about the very end of time because just two verses before (Daniel 12:2) he is talking about the rapture and everlasting life and everlasting condemnation.

The increase of knowledge is going both ways. Both the kingdoms of good and of evil are being increased in knowledge. We have seen knowledge being increased in the last 120 years in technology. But I believe great visions of the Kingdom of God are available to us now even as they were to Daniel in the sixth century. We just need to position ourselves as Daniel positioned himself. That was the reason the book of Daniel was written. God wanted to show us an example of how to function in captivity and not be completely taken over.

Jesus knew these days were coming, therefore he said,

And accept those days be shortened there should be no flesh be saved but for the elect sake those they shall be shortened.

—Matthew 24:22

Jesus also wondered:

Nevertheless when the son of man cometh shall he find faith in the Earth?

—Luke 18:8

God wants you to know this information that you are reading in here. God wants you to be aware. He wants your eyes opened. He wants you to be diligent. He wants you to be intelligent. In Hosea, God says,

My people are destroyed for lack of knowledge…

—Hosea 4:6a

It is not God's will that you would be destroyed because of lack of this information. I'll say it again, In Daniel 12:4, the angel tells Daniel to close the book, but in Revelation 22:10, the angel tells John to open the book. This is the season that we must get spiritual knowledge and understanding like Daniel. How did he glean such knowledge? It was through fasting and prayer. We must remember Daniel!

OVERTAKE!

Where art thou? During the times of Daniel, King Nebuchadnezzar came in and besieged Judah. He besieged it. What is happening today?

That time was truly a time of trouble and rebuke and blaspheme. Where was David to rebuke Nebuchadnezzar as he had done to Goliath? How dare Nebuchadnezzar come against the apple of God's eye in the city of the great king! Surely it was a time of blasphemy to the name of the Lord. King Nebuchadnezzar came in and took the vessels of the Lord. Can you imagine? Both types of vessels—the people and the furniture in the house of God. Blasphemy! The enemy came into Jerusalem to overtake it, and Judah had no strength in them to restrain them. David was nowhere to be found. It was a different time. The time would not have permitted David. It was the fullness of time for God's wrath upon Judah. David couldn't have helped. No one could have.

The Jews were weakened by the power of their sins. They were weakened by the power of their compromise. They were weakened by their disobedience unto the Lord. They had to say amen to their captivity. Daniel, on the other hand, was just along for the ride. He was amid the captivity but was not captured. Jesus shows us a truth:

> *I have given them thy word; and the world hath hated them, because they are not of the world, even as I am not of the world. I pray not that thou shouldest take them out of the world, but that thou shouldest keep them from the evil.*

> —John 17:14–15 (emphasis mine)

One question we may ask is, Why was Daniel among them in captivity? According to this conversation that Jesus is having with the Father concerning His disciples, we can conclude it was God's will for Daniel to remain among them. There was a purpose for Daniel's presence in the very midst of the chaos. Daniel was there just as we are on the earth to be a light today. Jesus helps us to understand that it's His desire to keep us here and for such an appointed time. Even as Daniel knew he was not in complete submersion, we must remember that for ourselves also.

CAPTIVATED BY THE INTERNET

Judah was forced to take a journey from Jerusalem to about 500 miles away to get to Babylon, their place of captivity. This must have been a difficult journey. It was without an airplane or a car or even a bicycle. Unfortunately, the lack of a vehicle was not the most difficult part of the trip. The main problem was not the physical passage as much as it was the hardship of leaving their own place to go serve another master. It was a spiritual journey of going into bondage.

The trip that Adam and Eve took out of the Garden of Eden was probably just as difficult, if not more so. To leave your place of blessing and belonging is not easy, but Adam and Eve had to leave their place because of disobedience, just as Judah did.

> *Therefore the Lord God sent forth from the Garden of Eden to till the ground from whence he was taken. He so he drove out the man and he placed at the east of the Garden of Eden cherubims. And a flaming sword which turned every way to keep the way of the tree of life.*
>
> —Genesis 3:23–24

God asked Adam a popular question in the Genesis 3: "Where are you?" God knew that Adam had left where he was, and he had transformed into the land of captivity in the spirit. Adam's body, soul, and spirit was transformed to a different place. God felt the transformation. He felt the shift just as Jesus felt it when the woman with the issue of blood received life into her body. God felt the death that happened with Adam and Eve. He felt the disconnection. He felt the travel; the translation.

The place of captivity has a completely different atmosphere. They felt naked. Adam was not clothed and did not feel the comfort that he once had. He looked for leaves to cover himself because he was exposed to a different atmosphere. In the natural, Adam had to leave the Garden of Eden and be barred from it. He was not able to take any more of the blessings in Eden. He was not fit for the same atmosphere anymore. The relationship had changed between him and God. We find this to be true in Revelation; as the third angel preaches the third message, it reads,

And the third angel followed them, saying with a loud voice, If any man worship the beast and his image, and receive his mark in his forehead, or in his hand, The same shall drink of the wine of the wrath of God, which is poured out without mixture into the cup of his indignation; and he shall be tormented with fire and brimstone in the presence of the holy angels, and in the presence of the Lamb.

—Revelation 14:9–10

Isn't this the same as in Genesis?

But of the tree of the knowledge of good and evil, thou shalt not eat of it: for in the day that thou eatest thereof thou shalt surely die.

—Genesis 3:17

Wow! In Revelation 14:9, God warns us not to worship the beast or receive his mark, or we will suffer the wrath of God.

Why would God say that? This is because at the beginning, God warned us about eating from the forbidden fruit, but we did. Once we did, we changed alliances. In the same way, whoever worships the beast will change alliances from God to beast and must suffer damnation to hell. This is very serious.

Reading the book of Revelation and doing what it says is a very serious matter. It shows us so.

Blessed is he that readeth, and they that hear the words of this prophecy, and keep those things which are written therein: for the time is at hand.

—Revelation 1:3

Once you belong to another, you must be separated and completely cut off from God because He is holy. Adam was cut off and was in captivity, outside of the Garden of Eden. Captivity is a spiritual place that we travel to because of disobedience. God has the rules; He made them. He knows why he made them, and He asked that we follow them. When we do not follow them, we then travel into captivity.

God always has a remnant. Though the children of Israel were confined in Babylon, God had a remnant. Daniel, Hananiah, Mishael, and Azariah were part of His remnant there. These four were living in a crooked and perverse nation, just as Paul talks about in Philippians 2.

What about you? Do you feel that you live amid a crooked nation or generation today? Do you have the integrity of Daniel? Are you able to sustain your faith under the temptation of bowing down to this world's image? Are you able to pray at any time that you would like to pray? If you can't, that's captivity. Help us, Lord.

That last question is harder and trickier than we think. By conspiracy of his colleagues, Daniel was placed in a position that he was not able to pray when he desired to pray. But he prayed anyway by his determination. Do we get in that situation today? Let me explain. Though it may seem we don't have a natural conspiracy against our prayer life, there is a spiritual one. I'm sure we can all admit there are times that it's difficult to pray. That's the spirit of the Babylonian system coming against us, which is the spirit of this world. How does he come? He comes with the lust of the flesh, the lust of the eyes, and the pride of this life. These things were offered to Daniel all the time. He had amazing self-control and didn't say yes to every gift, especially the pride of life.

It seems sometimes there are so many other things to do or think about than prayer. At times we may get sleepy when it's time to pray. Of course, praying in the open, as Daniel did, is yet another challenge altogether. It's important to know that spiritual wickedness is at work against our prayer life. There is a conspiracy in the spirit realm that hinders us from being free or able to pray. That is indeed a weapon formed in the spirit realm. It's the spirit of wickedness in high places.

We want to be like Daniel and be able to get on our knees three times a day and pray, but there's an intimidation that stands in front of us. If we pray when we want to pray, we can sometimes feel the resistance.

Are you in captivity? It's time to be set free! I find fasting to be a great help. That was Daniel's big secret weapon.

TAKEN

I watched a movie years ago called *Taken*. In the movie, a daughter and her friend were exhilarated to go to Europe, but her father was very leery about letting her go. She insisted, and because she was so eager about it, he let her go. She had an appetite! She did not take into consideration the father's concern. In her ignorance, excitement, and her fleshly appetite, she fell into captivity. That is the very thing that happens to us sometimes.

Living life and not paying attention to the Father's heart and His concerns about us, we can forget that the Father knows better for us. As the girl in the movie felt or discerned the eyes of the kidnapper, she looked for a place to hide. Psalm 91 tells us where and how to hide. In that first verse we are told to hide in God's secret place by abiding under His shadow. His shadow is His protection and presence. We must stay there. She looked around to find a place to hide because she felt exposed, just as Adam looked around to find something to hide his nakedness. But it was too late for either of them—both were captured. It was too late for Adam to come out of captivity on his own. He needed the Father's help. So the Father, our Father, has sent Jesus Christ to bring us out of captivity. We are covered by His blood. We are hidden with Christ.

For ye are dead, and your life is hid with Christ in God.

—Colossians 3:3

We just learned in the book of Daniel that the children of Israel were taken into captivity; just ask Adam, Judah, and the young lady in the movie. It was because of their appetite for the things that the Father warned them of. The children of Israel were functioning in their emotions, and they just kept going after other fleshly desires, things that looked good to the soul, things that looked more comfortable. They would not stay in the barricades, or God's safety nets, so they got caught in the enemy's net. The safety of God is the laws of God. The children of Israel did not take into consideration that they were set apart; they forgot about their God and were listening to other gods. Ultimately, their disobedience carried them into the hands of the enemy.

WHAT DOES SPIRITUAL CAPTIVITY LOOK LIKE?

Most of us don't think about captivity in the possibility of body, soul, or spirit. We visualize imprisonment to be physical only, which leaves possibilities for us to walk around living our lives and thinking everything is okay. The fact is, we may be in captivity and not know it. This is precisely what Jesus was saying in Matthew.

> *But as the days of Noah were, so shall also the coming of the Son of man be. For as in the days that were before the flood they were eating and drinking, marrying and giving in marriage, until the day that Noe entered into the ark, And knew not until the flood came, and took them all away; so shall also the coming of the Son of man be.*

> —Matthew 24:37–39

In Revelation 3, as Jesus speaks to the last church, the church of Laodicea, he tells them that they are lukewarm. They had no idea they didn't have enough fire. In Matthew 25, the ten foolish virgins were clueless about extra oil until it was too late. Most times, we have bonds and chains on us that we have no knowledge of. Daniel was in captivity but not of soul and spirit. It took a harlot named Delilah to lure Samson into captivity, and was it body, soul, and spirit?

> *And she said, The Philistines be upon thee, Samson. And he awoke out of his sleep, and said, I will go out as at other times before, and shake myself. And he wist not that the Lord was departed from him. But the Philistines took him, and put out his eyes, and brought him down to Gaza, and bound him with fetters of brass; and he did grind in the prison house.*

> —Judges 16:20–21

When Samson woke up, he had no idea that he had been in captivity. The Bible says he went to shake himself as he was used to, and he realized his power was gone. Samson was flowing in his emotions for Delilah, so he was not paying attention to his assignment. He was captured by the Philistines. He forgot who he was. He was not sober; he was relaxed and fell into captivity. This is hardly different from what happened with Adam and Eve.

Eve allowed her imagination and her heart to be captured by Satan. It wasn't until afterward that they realized that they were in trouble. Like Samson, immediately after compromising, they knew something was different. Why are we talking about this? It's because I believe we live in a day of time where we must be very careful and mindful of where we are. God asked Adam, Where are you? That was the first thing He asked. In the journey that Adam was on with God, he had plateaued in his relationship. He was in a place where he was not able to continue the intimacy that he had with God before that sin. Eventually, it led to a place of captivity. The captivity of Adam and Eve was of body, soul, and spirit. It was death.

Judah was in captivity in their soul, which is their mind and their heart. They yielded their spirit to other gods, and their spirit was eventually consumed in the natural, in their physical bodies.

There were warnings after warnings by the prophets to stop their spiritual adultery with the other gods, but their hearts were hardened. Their minds, or their souls, would not make a decision. Eventually, King Nebuchadnezzar came and took them into captivity even of their bodies.

Are you paying attention to how popular tattoos are these days? Yes, there have always been tattoos, but in the past few years, have you not noticed the increase? It's almost as if it were a physical manifestation of soul or spirit captivity. Before you shut this idea down, think of the purpose of tattoos and what the word of God says about them. I have asked dozens of people about their tattoos. The most popular response I get is their connection to that particular image or words. The scary thing is that many tattoos are demonic by sight. Most of them are deities, reptiles, or weird graphics. Also, the most popular location on the body for these tattoos are around the neck or on a limb. There are some that connect the person to a dead loved one or some type of a soul tie. God commands us,

> *Ye shall not make any cuttings in your flesh for the dead, nor print any marks upon you: I am the Lord.*
>
> —Leviticus 19:28

PLACES OF CAPTIVITY

It is now time to talk about the "where." In the scenario of Jerusalem's captivity, the place was Jerusalem. In our day the place is the globe, but to be more specific, our bodies. There is a global agenda at hand, and we find it in Revelation 13. We are body, soul, and spirit. The enemy desires to overtake us in all three areas. Yes, he does! That was his plan with Daniel, Meshach, Shadrack, Abednego, and the rest.

In our generation, He wants the world—every nation, every tongue, every tribe, every person to our very body, soul, and spirit. Let's be like Daniel and his three companions—let's remember who our God is and who we belong to. Though this world has its agenda, we must remember that our names are written in the Lamb's Book of Life from the foundation of the world. Daniel kept that in mind.

> *And it was given unto him to make war with the saints, and to overcome them: and power was given him over all kindreds, and tongues, and nations. And all that dwell upon the earth shall worship him, whose names are not written*

in the book of life of the Lamb slain from the foundation of the world.

—Revelation 13:7–8

According to these scriptures, we are in danger of total captivity. In this hour, the churches are influenced and shut down by plans of the enemy. Are we in captivity even now? What do you think? In the days of Jerusalem's captivity, Nebuchadnezzar did not only overtake the city of Jerusalem, but he also took the vessels. Vessels, as we understand in 2 Timothy 2:20, are our bodies. It reads:

But in a great house there are not only vessels of gold and of silver, but also of wood and of earth; and some to honour, and some to dishonour. Therefore if anyone cleanses himself from the latter, he will be a vessel for honor, sanctified and useful for the Master, prepared for every good work.

—2 Timothy 2:20–21

The enemy desires to overtake our very body, which is the temple of the Holy Spirit. He wants to defile it. Daniel would not allow that. What about me and you? Will we? What is your place of captivity?

Jesus says,

If the Son therefore shall make you free, ye shall be free indeed.

—John 8:36

How free are you? For some of us, captivity is very obvious, but for others, it's unclear. That vague place is dangerous because you don't know that you need help. If we are bound in drugs or alcohol, then it's obvious that we are being held captive. But if we don't have a situation in our life that is obvious, then we can easily fall into the deception that we don't need to be saved from bondage. Apostle Paul says,

> *Wherefore let him that thinketh he standeth take heed lest he fall.*

> —1 Corinthians 10:12

It's very important to check on our hearts daily. The captivity that came to Jerusalem happened because their hearts were turned.

The scriptures tell us even the earth is in bondage from the disobedience of Adam and Eve. We must be set free because, believe it or not, creation awaits our manifestation since it was made subject to vanity because of us. Yes, all of creation is in captivity to a certain extent.

> *For the earnest expectation of the creature waiteth for the manifestation of the sons of God. For the creature was made subject to vanity, not willingly, but by reason of him who hath subjected the same in hope, Because the creature itself also shall be delivered from the bondage of corruption into the glorious liberty of the children of God. For we know that the whole creation groaneth and travaileth in pain together until now.*

> —Romans 8:19–22

They were completely barred from the garden.

How Did We Become Captives?

First, let's consider the fact that there are different levels of spiritual captivity. In the Garden of Eden, Satan captivated Eve's attention and wisely brought her and her husband to captivity. How deeply were they captured? We can at least assume deeply enough that God had to exile them from the garden. From that time humanity has been struggling with different levels of captivity. During the exile Daniel was at a lesser level of captivity than some others. We know this because he was often set apart from the rest of the captives.

Judah was in sin for many years. The compromise of her relationship with God caused her to be vulnerable. Her vulnerability led her to be harassed by foreign nations for many years. God kept enough of a hedge of protection around His people to keep them from being completely destroyed, but He also kept warning them about their wickedness.

God allowed King Nebuchadnezzar to exile them from their native nation. Google describes the word "exile" as "having been expelled and barred from one's native country, typically for political or punitive reasons."

Adam and Eve were exiled from the Garden of Eden in Genesis chapter 3.

Getting captured is a process. Both in Adam and Eve's case and in the children of Israel's case, we find that it took a time of some compromise. According to the many stories we read of the prophets, we find that God was extremely patient before allowing His people to get captured and exiled. The journey into spiritual captivity does not happen overnight; it is an actual journey.

We serve a loving God, a loving Father that wants our safety. He wants us to be safe. God knows better for us, He knows where the dangers are, and He knows the end from the beginning of a thing. He set the rules and knows how they work. The Word of God is our standard.

In Exodus 20, God gave the children of Israel the Ten Commandments. One of those commandments is to not have any other gods before Him. Every sin that we do is in connection to serving another master. We go into captivity because we ignore the laws of God. God tells us in his Word over and over to walk in his ways, his statutes, and his wisdom. We must fight our own desires and walk in His ways to stay out of captivity. We are enticed to compromise; therefore, there's something about the human heart that wants to do what it's not supposed to do. It's a battle for us to keep rules and regulations. God pleads with us all the time to stay in his Word. Though the spirit is willing, the flesh is weak.

But I see you know the law in my members, warning against the law of my mind, and bringing me into captivity to the law of sin which is in my members.

—Romans 7:23

In the United States of America, the governmental system houses rules and regulations, and if those rules are broken, there are consequences. You may end up in jail if you don't control your behavior. When the police come, they look for evidence of who's at fault. Once they find fault, then the person is handcuffed and taken into captivity.

The way to know how we got into prison is to look at our rules. King Josiah understood that very well. When the priest read the laws of God to him, he realized they were far from them. He tried to stop the coming captivity. He represented going back to the laws of God. Unfortunately, the kings before him and the kings after him were not as wise.

We must make a choice and focus as Daniel did. Joshua was also focused. He understood a decision must be made in order to continue on to get to our destination, heaven. This earth is not our destination. The captivity of Jerusalem was necessary but wasn't God's desire. The captivity of your soul, your body, or your spirit may come, but it is not

God's desire. God's heart and desire is that we live in freedom and see the New Jerusalem.

Joshua said,

> *...choose you this day whom ye will serve; whether the gods which your fathers served that were on the other side of the flood, or the gods of the Amorites, in whose land ye dwell: but as for me and my house, we will serve the Lord.*

—Joshua 24:15

During that period, Joshua noticed the lack of fear of the Lord, the lack of sincerity, and lack of truth. They had the gods, which their fathers served on the other side of the flood in Egypt.

We can surrender to God, or we can surrender to the enemy. Let's throw that white flag of surrender unto the Lord. Surrender to the enemy was never intended by God. That level of trust only belongs to Jesus Christ: to surrender and to be broken before Him. In conclusion, what do we do now? To stay out of captivity and to avoid complete imprisonment of body, soul, and spirit, we must pray as Daniel prayed. We must live a fasting life as he did. We must be bold and not compromise with this world. We have to pray, listen, and watch. We must get set free of the bondages of this world and pledge our allegiance to God alone. The book of Daniel is an example that we do not have to be in captivity even if the rest of the world is. Amen!

CHAPTER FIVE

DON'T FORGET THE DAYS OF NOAH

NOAH'S DAYS

5 And God saw that the **wickedness of man was great** in the earth, and that **every imagination of the thoughts** of his **heart** was only evil continually.

6 And it repented the Lord that he had made man on the earth, and it grieved him at his heart.

7 And the Lord said, I will destroy man whom I have created from the face of the earth; both man, and beast, and the creeping thing, and the fowls of the air; for it repenteth me that I have made them.

8   *But Noah found grace in the eyes of the Lord.*

                                                  —Genesis 6:5–8

AS THE DAYS OF NOAH WERE

36   *But of that day and hour knoweth no man, no, not the angels of heaven, but my Father only.*

37   *But as the days of Noah were, **so shall also the coming of the Son of man be**.*

38   *For as in the days that were before the flood they were eating and drinking, marrying and giving in marriage, until the day that Noe entered into the ark,*

39   *And knew not until the flood came, and took them all away; so shall also the coming of the Son of man*

                                         —Matthew 24:36–39

DAYS OF NOAH, LOT, AND LOT'S WIFE

26   *And as it was in the days of Noe, so shall it be also in the days of the Son of man be.*

27   *They did eat, they drank, they married wives, they were given in marriage, until the day that Noah entered into the ark, and the flood came, and destroyed them all.*

28   *Likewise also as it was in the days of Lot; they did eat, they drank, they bought, they sold, they planted, they builded;*

29 *But the same day that Lot went out of Sodom it rained fire and brimstone from heaven, and destroyed them all.*

30 *Even thus shall it be in the day when the Son of man is revealed.*

31 *In that day, he which shall be upon the housetop, and his stuff in the house, let him not come down to take it away: and he that is in the field, let him likewise not return back.*

32 *Remember Lot's wife.*

33 *Whosoever shall seek to save his life shall lose it; and whosoever shall lose his life shall preserve it..*

—Luke 17:26–33

AS WE REMEMBER Daniel, we must not forget the days of Noah because Jesus mentioned him also. Jesus pointed out the importance of Noah's time in relation to the last days. Jesus wants us to be aware. He wants us to remember. The Greek word for remember is *thymamai,* which also means recall and recollect. We are to recollect information of the past as we keep watch of the end time.

There are several characters of the Old Testament that Jesus asks that we pay attention to. In fact, in Luke 17:32 Jesus said plainly, "Remember Lot's wife." This is a warning. A warning we must pay attention to. The verse is simply three words but carry great value. What happened to her? Genesis chapter 19:26 tells us that Lot's wife looked back.

24 *Then the Lord rained upon Sodom and upon Gomorrah brimstone and fire from the Lord out of heaven;*

25 And he overthrew those cities, and all the plain, and all the inhabitants of the cities, and that which grew upon the ground.

26 But his wife looked back from behind him, and she became a pillar of salt.

—Genesis 19:24–26

In the midst of the destruction of Sodom and Gomorrah, she turned to look and became a pillar of salt. In just one verse we can see much about Lot's wife. Verse 26 does not say her name but associates her to her husband. In that same verse we can see her position. She was behind Lot. Could this mean that her heart was not on the same page as Lot? Looking back, she turned into a pillar of salt. It seems that she looked back in regret. Maybe her heart was melting as she watched the destruction of her life in the city. Her emotion deceived her. Right after Jesus told the disciples to remember Lot's wife, He says, *"Whosoever shall seek to save his life shall lose it; and whosoever shall lose his life shall preserve it"* (Luke 17:33).

In the end times many will be emotional about their stuff and will lose their salvation. It's a warning for the end-time Church to not attach our hearts to our stuff, the comforts of this world. Lot's wife was not able to completely turn her back on Sodom and Gomorrah. Perhaps she wanted one last peek. Maybe she forget to grab her favorite piece of jewelry.

Later on we will discuss the rising of the Antichrist, which will produce the whole world to be as Sodom and Gomorrah. Jesus tells us when we see the abomination of desolation sitting in the holy place to run to the mountains, stay put on the housetops, and to not turn back go get our stuff. Wow!

The writings of the Bible are left as a guide for you and me. No one knows the exact day or hour except God. In His last teachings to the disciples, Jesus took the time to give clues and warnings about the last days. Though He knew the disciples would not be alive during the very end of the days, He still found it important to do so. He knew you and I would read the writings of the disciples. We are expected to study God's Word. There are hidden clues, warnings, and treasures in it. Jesus expected Nicodemus to have had knowledge of God's Word because he was supposed to be a student and teacher of the Word of God. Just the same, Jesus expected the disciples to be familiar with the writings of Daniel and the prophecies of prophet Jeremiah. That's why He quoted the Old Testament during His teachings on several occasions.

WARNINGS AND CLUES TO US

Warnings and clues are a big part of understanding God's prophetic time clock. Jesus gave us clues and warnings because many will be deceived. The subject of the last days and the second coming of Jesus Christ is a crucial one. It's one we don't want to be deceived about, yet it's one that is easy to be deceived about. There is a lot in the Bible about this.

There are many keys in the book of Daniel concerning the last days. From Daniel's life circumstances, his visions, and his dreams, we can understand some of the activities that will be taking place on the earth leading up to the last days and even to the second coming of Christ. We explored his life in the first few chapters of this book to glean insight on him.

Daniel was indeed very impressive in character, yet the most impressive of all of his accomplishments is that Jesus himself acknowledged his prophecy in Matthew chapter 24:15. The activities of Daniel's day will help us to recognize the timing in our day. It's interesting that Jesus mentioned Daniel, Noah, Lot, and Lot's wife as he taught about the end of the days.

The last chapter of Daniel mentions the rapture of humanity from the earth. The angel describes the destiny of man as "some to everlasting life, and some to shame and everlasting contempt." As we continue to connect the dots and find warnings and clues, we find that Jesus, in Matthew 24, connects Noah to His second coming. The story of Noah is from the book of Genesis. Matthew 24:37–39 reads,

37 But as the days of Noah were, so shall also the coming of the Son of man be.

38 For as in the days that were before the flood they were eating and drinking, marrying and giving in marriage, until the day that Noe entered into the ark,

39 And knew not until the flood came, and took them all away; so shall also the coming of the Son of be.

—Matthew 24:37–39

As we all know, His second coming is the grand finale, yet He mentions a story from the very first book of the Bible. Interesting that Jesus refers to His second coming as "that day," and tells us that it's a day that no one knows. According to these passages it seems normal people will live life as normal. Well at least it will be their normal, yet their live gas been subtly altered. According to Matthew's and Luke's account most people will have no clue. The Bible tells us that they are eating, drinking, marrying, and giving into marriage and suddenly the Son of Man will be revealed. The book of Revelation is the revelation of Jesus Christ (Revelation 1:1).

THE SONS OF GOD AND THE DAUGHTERS OF MAN (A I)

Since the days of Adam and Eve there have been interference with God's creation, mankind. Artificial intelligence is the vehicle by which humanity is being compromised today.

1   *And it came to pass, when men began to multiply on the face of the earth, and daughters were born unto them,*

2   *That **the sons of God saw the daughters of men** that they were fair; and they took them wives of all which they chose.*

3   *And the Lord said, My spirit shall not always strive with man, for that he also is flesh: yet his days shall be an hundred and twenty years.*

4   *There were giants in the earth in those days; and also after that, when the sons of God came in unto the daughters of men, and they bare children to them, the same became mighty men which were of old, men of renown. And God saw that the wickedness of man was great in the earth, and that every imagination of the thoughts of his heart was only evil continually.*

—Genesis 6:1–5

God was watching as the sons of God, also known as the fallen angels, were interfering with God's plans for mankind. They were called the sons of God because they were created by God, as He created all beings. In Genesis 3, we read about the serpent that was subtler than any beast of the field that God created. Don't let that throw you off. God created the adversary. But if we take heed of His warnings and do what He tells us to do, we have nothing to worry about. Isaiah 54:17 tells us no weapon formed against us shall prosper. The verse prior says God created the destroyer. God gives us all this information so that we are aware. He is in control.

In Genesis 6:4, the offspring of the sons of God (fallen angels) and the daughters of man (regular humans) are called giants. Keep in mind when we see "daughters of man" don't assume it's only of the female gender. It can be translated to simply "humans." It were those giants the twelve spies that Moses sent out to spy the land of Canaan in Numbers 13 were afraid of. When they came back, only Caleb and Joshua had the faith to see the giants could be conquered, just like only Daniel and his friends were able to stand up against the influence of Babylon. The daughters of men were like the other spies that went with Joshua and Caleb—they didn't have the strength. Such beings are easily conquered and overtaken.

But remember God always has His remnants. Joshua and Caleb were the remnant in the book of Numbers that had the faith to stand up to the giants and believe God. Noah and his family were that remnant in Genesis 6. In the days of Daniel, he—and all of Jerusalem—was besieged into captivity, but Daniel and his friends were the remnant that would not bow their knees to the conformation of Babylon's kingdom. Today, you and I are it. In Luke 18:8, Jesus asked if He would find faith on the earth when he returns. You and I are the remnant in our generation. Or are we? If you are not, then maybe this book will help you to take heed of the lessons in the Bible and be vigilant.

Genesis 6:2 uses very interesting language. It sounds like the sons of God did not take just a few wives but as many as they wanted. It also seems like there was some raping going on. It was their choice. Were there some open doors in their lives that allowed the sons of God to come in and overtake them? It seems that there was a rapid growth happening, which we will come to understand better later in this chapter.

Evidently the depth of the evil in the days of Noah came from the interaction of fallen angels with humans. This was similar to Satan's interference with mankind in the garden of Eden. But what about now? What about our generation? You must really give this some thought.

Can there be an interference between humans and the realm that is not physical in this 21st century?

> *And it came to pass, when men began to multiply on the face of the earth, and daughters were born unto them, That the sons of God saw the daughters of men that they were fair; and they took them wives of all which they chose. And the Lord said, My spirit shall not always strive with man, for that he also is flesh: yet his days shall be an hundred and twenty years. There were giants in the earth in those days; and also after that, when the sons of God came in unto the daughters of men, and they bare children to them, the same became mighty men which were of old, men of renown. And God saw that the wickedness of man was great in the earth, and that every imagination of the thoughts of his heart was only evil continually.*
>
> —Genesis 6:1–5

What was significant in the days of Noah that Jesus was pointing out to us? In the days of Noah the whole human race was consumed under water except for the remnant, which was Noah and his family.

He describes a very relaxed time of living upon the earth. The interesting words were "drinking," "marrying," and "giving in marriage." We know it's a time where people are not sober; rather, they are intoxicated. They are marrying, so emotion is at an all-time high. And they are being handed over to be married. When we see the word "marriage" in the Bible it does not necessarily mean a man and a woman dressed in a tuxedo and a wedding dress in front of a priest or pastor saying their vows. Most times when we see the word "mar riage" in the Bible it generally indicates a covenant relation ship of some kind. In conclusion, there will be intimacy in relationship with covenant bonds that will be formed beyond one's own will. I also believe this happened to the women in Genesis chapter 6. I do believe there were some open doors in their lives to allow the invasion of these relationships. Why? Scripture proves that God is just and would not just allow such an invasion, unless we somehow, in the slightest way, give an open door to the intruder. Besides, **Genesis 6:9** tells us, *".... Noah was a just man and perfect in his generations, and Noah walked with God."* He was not in captivity. This sets Noah apart as one that didn't have come compromise to the enemy.

In Genesis chapter 6 the sons of God took as many wives as they wanted. Now, I'm not saying this overtaking happens without reason, but they sound somewhat forceful. There are situations in life sometimes that happen to us by invitation, whether it be through ignorance or whatever. Sometimes things happen and go further than we wanted to. This is the type of marriage I believe Jesus is talking about here in Matthew 24:38. There will be some of us that will enter covenant relationships in the spirit realm and other realms beyond our full consent. The enemy only needs a small opening to enter.

I believe we live in a time where there are plenty of opportunities for the enemy to enter our lives. The enemy has access to our souls through television, social media, food, entertainment, wrong relationships, fleshly desires, and so on.

This book that you are reading is a warning. Jesus took time to warn and prepare us in Matthew 24, Luke 21, Luke 17, and in several other passages. In Proverbs, we're told that warning comes before destruction. It also says if we have a haughty spirit, we will fall.

I do pray that all of us, including myself, take heed of the information in this book. I pray that we get the revelation that's in the Bible as a wake-up call. I pray that we do remember Daniel and the life that he lived even during captivity. Daniel's life was as if he were living right in the middle of the days of Noah. Noah's day was a time of trans humanism, and we see this in Daniel's time too when King Nebuchadnezzar sent Ashpenaz to choose certain children to be engineered to become a superhuman race.

The evil of the times of Noah that Jesus spoke about can only be overcome as we live the way Daniel lived. Why do you think Daniel was careful about eating from the king's table? We must learn from Daniel.

Adam was warned, yet he did not heed the warning. In the garden of Eden, Adam and Eve were influenced by the realm of the spirit, and they ate a fruit that was not supposed to be eaten. What was it that Satan promised Eve to interest her to take that first bite?

> *Now the serpent was more subtil than any beast of the field which the Lord God had made. And he said unto the woman, Yea, hath God said, Ye shall not eat of every tree of the garden? And the woman said unto the serpent, We may eat of the fruit of the trees of the garden: But of the fruit of the tree which is in the midst of the garden, God hath said, Ye shall not eat of it, neither shall ye touch it, lest ye die. And the serpent said unto the woman, **Ye shall not surely die:** For God doth know that in the day ye eat thereof, then your eyes shall be opened, and **ye shall be as gods**, **knowing** good and evil. And when the woman saw that the tree was good for food, and that it was pleasant to the eyes, and a tree to be desired to make one wise, she took of the fruit thereof, and did eat, and gave also unto her husband with her; and he did eat. And the eyes of them both were opened, and they knew that they were naked; and they sewed fig leaves together, and made themselves aprons.*
>
> —Genesis 3:1–7 (emphasis mine)

Lucifer worked a plan to destroy Adam and Eve. He first asked her a question to get her to bring her into confusion about what God said. He then lied to her by telling her she would not die. Then he told her that she would in fact be like gods. Finally, he told her that she would have knowl edge; basically, he told her that she would have superpowers.

Obviously, Satan was trying to convince her she was infe rior to other beings. He was also telling her the powers that God had given her were just not enough, and she needed more. She needed to be a superhuman, which leads to trans humanism. The fruit the serpent convinced Adam and Eve to eat changed them from what God originally intended them to be. Did you notice that one of the things that was offered was power, which would change their very beings? Did you notice another was knowledge? Knowledge!

THE INTELLECTUAL BREED

Both the book of Daniel and the book of Revelation are full of symbols, numbers, images, and visions. In the collec tion of all of these, there is an awareness of timing and knowl edge. In Daniel 12:4 the two are mentioned in one verse.

> ...But thou, O Daniel, shut up the words, and seal the book, even to **the time** of the end: many shall run to and fro, and **knowledge** shall be increased.
>
> —Daniel 12:4

Daniel, Shadrach, Meshach, and Abednego were part of the scholarly type of young men during the captivity of Judah in Babylon. It was the intent of King Nebuchadnezzar to raise up an intellectual breed of man, and he asked for off spring meeting certain criteria to be brought in to be trained. Daniel's age at that time would fit in our Generation Z age group of today (ages 11–26). The king was looking for young, tender minds that he could form and conform to his agenda. What agenda was that?

One can imagine that Nebuchadnezzar, in his pride, felt as the king of the superpower of the world, he must engi neer others to stand as superiors in his kingdom. His atti tude becomes quite evident in the third chapter of Daniel. Today, we are experiencing the same thing but at a higher level and a faster pace. It seems now that even babies are born with higher levels of intelligence than in the past. That change is due to technology and the ever-so-silent modifica tion of mankind.

At just a few months old, babies have a connection with cell phones. Is it just the bright shining light? It seems more than that. To take it a bit further, younger people (Generation Z) are better able to understand the operations of cell phone devices. When it comes to electronics, they are more intelli gent than the older generations (Generation X, baby boom-ers, or the silent generation). The most popular candidates for computer programming are young people, such as millen nials. Their genes seem different. It's interesting that King Nebuchadnezzar asked for the young.

Scientists are hard at work, and their work is being dis played on movies. This is to let us know what comes next. They are confident of their discoveries through their studies. Through movies and other media they display their projects and plans.

It's amazing to see the things that were predicted and are now taking place today. I remember being a little girl and watching the cartoon *The Jetsons*. I enjoyed the show, but I never thought it would be possible to experience the modern technology they enjoyed because it didn't yet exist in our world. We thought it was just entertainment, and I enjoyed the futuristic show as if it were just a show. They had com puters, cell phones, space travel, and robotics. The dog had a treadmill. Traffic cops pressed buttons to look up offenders. Food came in the form of a pill. They cooked with a micro wave. They used modern medical technology like EEGs and MRIs. Mrs. Jetson would press a button for all her housework.

Their predictions even dictated human behaviors in the future. The wife's attitude in the cartoon was not at all "a humble wife"—she was materialistic and manipulative with her husband. This displays a great difference from what wives used to be in time past even from the early 1900s. We pay attention to such details because it shows the change as time advance. Also in *The Jetsons*, the daughter was not very respectful to her parents, as I'm sure many mothers of teenage daughters today can testify. Today we are living in *The Jetsons'* world. Humanity is changing and becoming more and more alienated from biblical teachings or godly wisdom.

More than 50 years ago, there was a group of scientists that met to put pieces of the puzzle together. They were making predictions of what would happen in the future to the world from where the world was then and if we continued that path.[1]

> *And God saw that the wickedness of man was great in the earth, and that every imagination of the thoughts of his heart was only evil continually.*
>
> —Genesis 6:5

They concluded that in the next 50 years, we would expe rience: controlled nuclear weapons, household robots, wide band wire communications, fertility control, life control, genetic control, opinion control, human-to-human trans mission, and so on. Maybe that's how the writers of *The Jetsons* got the ideas of where we would be today. If that's the case, then whatever is going to happen in the future has already been perceived or put together by scientist and other planners. Many movies have been made that have predicted things for the future years in advance.

In *The Jetsons*, even the attitudes of the people were dif ferent than the time that I was a child watching it, but we see these very attitudes today in families. The husband, George Jetson, is manipulated in the household and stressed at work. The wife, Jane, was a compulsive shop-

---

1   One, Reelblack, director. The Futurist (1967) Scientists Predict the 21st Century. YouTube, 15 Dec. 2018, https://youtu.be/wPETzKYLkco. Accessed 7 June 2022.

per, cold-hearted, and hated to cook. She uses artificial intelligence for all her housework. She has expense machines that do the cooking by just the pressing of a few buttons. Jane's fingers press to iron, vacuum, and wash clothes. She goes over George's head and video-calls her mother for advice when he disagrees. Kids are disrespectful to the parents and so on. There are other examples in the show that were not possible back then, but today we live them. In one episode, Mr. Jetson is dressed as a woman, and his wife compliments him. It's shocking to go back and watch these shows.

ARTIFICIAL INTELLIGENCE

Artificial intelligence, or AI, is the simulation or imitation of human intelligence processes by machines, especially computer systems. It is modeled on the human brain. It's a gigantic network of a hundred billion interconnection of wires somewhat like the specialized cell transmitting nerve system in the human brain. Science has been able to achieve this level of technology from a collection of physics and mathematical studies over the last few centuries. I believe we will, in the next hundred years, arrive on the top of a tech nological slope. It's scary to see the plans that science has for mankind at the peak.

There are several types of artificial intelligence: reactive, limited theory, theory of mind, and self-aware. Reactive AI reacts to existing conditions. Limited theory artificial intel ligence can absorb learning data and is widely used today in online learning tools. Theory of mind AI has the capability to understand and remember emotions and can replicate them. An example of this would be Sophia, the humanoid robot who was introduced in 2016. Self-aware AI refers to when machines can understand and remember emotions and can replicate and also be aware of their own emotions. They are also looking at going into artificial superintelligence, where the machines will be smarter than humans, and scientists are saying this level might take over the world. Scientists say AI might surpass human intelligence by 2030. This is just a few years from now. It's scary that they're even entertaining the possibility of age-reversal, which they hope will conquer death completely. Doesn't this sound like direct competition with God and complete rebellion?

We are looking at a generation of rebellion. What does rebelling have to do with artificial intelligence? Remember, the pursuit of greater intelligence is what convinced Eve to rebel in the first place.

And the serpent said unto the woman, Ye shall not surely die:

For God doth know that in the day ye eat thereof, then your eyes shall be opened, and yeshall be as gods, knowing good and evil.

—Genesis 3:4–5

Well, of course we know it was a lie that she would not die because she did. The next lie was that she would be like gods. The result was actually that she lost her relationship with the true God. Finally, he told her that she would have knowledge of good and evil, a big deception because nakedness made them uncomfortable.

After that untruth, her vision was changed. She was con vinced. We are living in these lies today as we touch artificial intelligence—the lies that we will be like gods. As we read and observe the conversation between Eve and the serpent, we must ask ourselves, What led Eve to rebel? What did the serpent promise her? Knowledge.

One of the perks that was promised to provoke the rebel lion was higher intelligence. Ladies and gentlemen, we are still fighting the same battle. Artificial intelligence is a direct slap in the face to God. It tells God we do not want to be human; we want to be superhuman. We want to be trans human. We will plug wires into us so that we can do things that our natural brain would not normally do. It's also saying we are willing to give our brain power over to electronics to dictate and manage us. How many people do we know wear an Apple watch to calculate their breathing, their sleep, their heart rate, and their everything? I was sitting next to a woman a few days ago, and she told me that her watch just reminded her to breathe. We are willing to give science our bodies even though Romans 12:1 tells us to present our bodies unto God. People, we are in trouble.

Artificial intelligence is intelligence that is different from what God has decided to give to us as human beings. The truth is, we become stupid as a computer takes over. Where is the computer getting the power? Interesting thought!

General Approaches to AI

Neuralink and Synchron are two popular companies that deal with brain-computer interface or brain-machine inter face. Basically, they implant devices in the body. According to Wikipedia, brain-computer interface, or BCI, "is a direct communication pathway between the brain's electrical activity and an external device, most commonly a computer or robotic limb." In the past, these surgeries were usually tested on monkeys, but in 2021, the FDA cleared Synchron's brain-computer interface device for human trials.

Companies such as Neuralink and Synchron have tech nology to help a person with amyotrophic lateral sclerosis (ALS), also called Lou Gehrig's disease. It's a disease of the nervous system where people lose the ability to speak or move. These companies have the ability to allow a person with ALS to control an electronic device with their brain. The BCI system functions like a bridge to bypass broken connec tions in the brain and body by placing electrode wires under the skull into the blood vessels of the brain that are connected to a computer or device. The device allows a paralyzed person to communicate by text through thought. This type of tech nology is the future of medicine.

Over the past decades, artificial intelligence has been used in many medical procedures. One example is artificial insem ination, or the deliberate introduction of sperm into a female cervix for pregnancy without intercourse, usually used by those that can't have kids or by homosexuals. These machines provide an opportunity for us to do what we want instead of submitting to God. When Hannah was barren, she humbled herself and cried out to God. She did not have access to a machine that would take away her shame.

Reproduction is very holy to God. After all, He did create humanity, so that's understandable, right? God was upset Onan spilled his sperm on the ground instead of allowing Tamar to get pregnant.

AUGMENTED REALITY

Augmented reality is an interactive experience over the real-world environment where the two objects that reside in the real world are augmented by computer-generated percep tual information, sometimes across multiple sensory modal ities. One example of this advanced technology is humans giving machines permission to type with their brain or move an object through the communication of the human brain and sensory wires.

Facebook is coming up with technologies that can read your mind. Facebook robots develop their own language technology with super strength.

Artificial tractors can graze crops; the machine knows the difference between a weed and a plant. Health care car robots are also in the works.

The name of the game with artificial intelligence is alter ation of God's creation or creature, especially the alteration of humans. That alteration comes in different forms such as drugs. One example is Ritalin. America takes about 90 per cent of the world's Ritalin. This drug is used to help focus. The problem with so many needing to take it is that God designed us to naturally be able to focus. Well, generally we know that drugs are already a problem today as the world gets more and more stressful or out of God's will. Human beings are restless these days. Some try to digitize all aspect of their lives, but that becomes a problem for the human body. Many wear an Apple watch or some type of device that calculates everything that their bodies do. That is sad.

THE DAY OF THE SON OF MAN—THE SECOND COMING

With all this talk about the time of the end, let us also understand that after the time of the end is the beginning of the new earth and New Jerusalem. Before this, there will be the second coming of our Lord Jesus Christ. Regarding the time of the end, Jesus says we won't know the day or the hour, but He does say that we'll know the signs.

One of the events signaling the time of the end is near will be the weather. Jesus told us this in Matthew 24:36, where He said there will be earthquakes. Are we not seeing this mani festation on the earth as weather all over the globe seems like it's going crazy? Of course, some of it is by design because the weather all over the globe is controlled by artificial intel ligence. We are aware of that as well. I find it interesting that a passage of scripture in Romans reads:

> For the earnest expectation of the creature waiteth for the manifestation of the sons of God. For the creature was made subject to vanity, not willingly, but by reason of him who hath subjected the same in hope, because the creature itself also shall be delivered from the bondage of corruption into the glorious liberty of the children of God.
>
> —Romans 8:19–21

In this passage, we are aware of the creature in its expec tation. What creature is that? The creature is all of God's creation. We do under-stand that God gave man power over animals and the ground to work it. In verse 20, it shows that the creature was made subject to vanity.

When someone or something is made "subject to" that means they have a master, someone or something driving them. So we find in this pas sage that vanity is the master of the creature. Vanity? Selah.

What are some ways that you can think of the earth being made subject to something? How about weapons that are made of the creature, such as iron turned into swords, guns, and other weapons of war? Gun powder and other substances are turned into explosions for war. That is beyond the crea ture's power. It is picked up and manipulated into whatever man decides (God gave Adam dominion). The creature was made subject to vanity when man sinned. The creature meaning the earth. In fact, the very earth was cursed as Adam and Eve were receiving their sentence. Humanity's behavior has put earth in bondage, and now earth awaits their mani festations so they can be taken out of bondage. Verse 21 tells us the creature itself also shall be delivered from bondage of corruption. Amen. Even so, come Lord Jesus, come.

In Luke 17:26–36, Jesus tells parables about His return. He reminds us about the days of Noah how the world was before the flood came and destroyed. He points out that everyone was eating and drinking and hav ing a good time. He then likens it to the day of Lot as he destroyed Sodom and Gomorrah with fire and brimstone. He points out how Lot and his family were taken as the cities were burning. Finally, in this passage, Jesus is warning us and informing us that there will be two people, and one will be taken and the other left. Wow, he gave us so many hints. It will be a shame if any of us are taken by surprise at the second coming of Jesus. Our Lord has given us all the warnings, clues, and the knowledge.

In Hosea, God says,

> My people are destroyed for lack of knowledge: because thou hast rejected knowledge, I will also reject thee, that thou shalt be no priest to me: seeing thou hast forgotten the law of thy God, I will also forget thy children.

—Hosea 4:6

God is not taking the blame for our lack of knowledge once he has given us the knowledge that we need. Yes, He is coming as a thief in the night, and we don't know the day or the hour, but we must be knowledgeable of the signs.

CHAPTER SIX

SOCIETIES TODAY

And the whole earth was of one language, and of one speech. And it came to pass, as they journeyed from the east, that they found a plain in the land of Shinar; and they dwelt there. And they said one to another, Go to, let us make brick, and burn them thoroughly. And they had brick for stone, and slime had they for morter. And they said, Go to, let us build us a city and a tower, whose top may reach unto heaven; and let us make us a name, lest we be scattered abroad upon the face of the whole earth. And the Lord came down to see the city and the tower, which the children of men builded.

—Genesis 11:1–5

THE FIRST MAN-MADE SOCIETY ON EARTH

IN ACTUALITY, THE first society on earth was Adam and Eve in the garden of Eden. God was the builder and maker of that society; it was to be a kingdom. A kingdom is a territory ruled by a king. God's vision for His society was that His crea ture would both enjoy His rulership and allow His rulership unto them. God's will was rulership with relation-ships. He loved His subjects, so His vision was not that of a dictatorship. God created the earth, placed man in the garden, and pro vided for them. It was a beautiful relationship between God and man for a period of time. The relationship was built on love and trust, yet it required obedience from man unto God.

Obedience has a component of dependency; the Creator did not create man to be self-sustaining. The serpent was aware of that truth and brought in a lie. Satan came with an offer of false self-reliance. Unfor-tunately, God's society took the bite. In this chapter, we're going to talk mainly about societies built by human beings. Let's look at the first man made society.

Nimrod

We find the first man-made society in the 11th chapter of Genesis. The Word of God tells us about the builder of that kingdom.

> *And Cush begat Nimrod: he began to be a mighty one in the earth. He was a mighty hunter before the Lord: wherefore it is said, Even as Nimrod the mighty hunter before the Lord. And the beginning of his kingdom was Babel, and Erech, and Accad, and Calneh, in the land of Shinar.*
>
> —Genesis 10:8–10

We find that the builder of that society was Nimrod. How did he come about? First, God created Adam and Eve and governed them in the garden, but they broke the law and were banned. In Genesis 5, we find the genealogy from Adam to Noah and his three sons. By

Genesis, chapter 6, the earth was full of evil activity and mighty men. God then called Noah to build an ark because he planned to destroy man from the face of the earth with a flood. Noah, his family, and a selection of animals went into the ark for salvation. After the flood, they were the only survivors on earth. Noah, his wife, his three sons, and their wives were the survivors. In Genesis 10 we find the genealogy of the families of the sons of Noah, and Nimrod was Cush's son, Noah's great-grandson.

Nimrod in Hebrew means "a skillful hunter." As a Hebrew boy's name, it also means "we will rebel." Does the name "Nimrod" sound familiar in today's world? It is used as a syn onym for "moron." If you were ever a Bugs Bunny cartoon fan, I'm sure you heard Bugs call Elmer Fudd, the hunter, "Nimrod," as he would outsmart the hunter from catching him.

There also appears to be another interesting connec tion between passages about Nimrod and another section of scripture. Isaiah 14 records a conversation that God had with Lucifer. Seems to me that Lucifer desired to ascend to the heavens even as Nimrod desired to ascend to the heavens.

> *For thou hast said in thine heart, I will ascend into heaven,*
> *I will exalt my throne above the stars of God: I will sit also*
> *upon the mount of the con gregation, in the sides of the north.*
>
> —Isaiah 14:43

NIMROD'S KINGDOM

Babel was the name of that first man-made society. In Hebrew, *babel* means "confusion." The place where they built the Tower of Babel was later called Babylon, located in the land of Shinar, which is mod-ern-day Iraq.

Nimrod was a hunter who aggregated all the people of the earth to live together in an ordered community. The unity in Nimrod's society was powerful. The kingdom initially consisted of Babel, Erech, Accad, and Calneh, in the land of Shinar.

We encounter this land of Shinar again in the sixth cen tury BC in the book of Daniel. In Daniel 1:2, we find that King Nebuchadnezzar brought the vessels of God from Jerusalem to the house of his gods in the land of Shinar. We know that he lived in great fear and paranoia. It may be because his gods lived in a place of confusion.

I also want to point out that Nebuchadnezzar was, as Nimrod, a great hunter and a mighty one on the earth. He was allowed to hunt the children of Israel and take them into captivity. He hunted the great young minds to conform them to his global agenda. In Genesis 11 the imagination of that agenda had to be stopped by God. God himself noticed this force. It was the force of unity and communication that Nimrod used to build his empire. Communication with unity is very powerful.

God resolved this situation by confounding their lan guage, which resulted in limiting Nimrod's kingdom.

I find the language used in Daniel 10:10 to be interesting because it says, "The beginning of his kingdom" and then names the kingdoms. I must point out that everything that has a beginning has an end. Therefore, I wonder if the kingdom of Nimrod has yet ended on earth today. I don't think it has.

Lawlessness

> *Don't let anyone deceive you in any way, for that day will not come until the **rebellion** occurs and **the man of lawlessness** is revealed, the man doomed to destruction.*
>
> —2 Thessalonians 2:3 (emphasis mine)

Genesis 11 has always been known as "the Tower of Babel chapter," about a time that the whole world was in one accord. One accord? Sounds great! But is it? Not if the agenda behind it is rebellion. The Word of God tells us that rebellion is like the sin of witchcraft in Samuel 15:23. Through witchcraft and rebellion, the imagination of man can move at a very rapid speed. Therefore, you must realize that the imagination of man was out of control in Genesis 11. God pointed that out in verse six.

Knowledge, communication, agreement, imagination, and unity are all powerful attributes for great achievements. However great and powerful these qualities can be, if they are in partnership with lawlessness, the results can be devas tating. God knew men had to be stopped in their project of building the Tower of Babel, a tower that would reach up to the heavens, fundamentally to arise and roommate with God. They had no right to do what they were doing. They had not consulted with God for such a visit. This was not the pur pose that God created men for. Yes, God wants relationships with men, but not in this way—God and man are not equals. Nimrod's attempt to build an empire to reach the heavens and Nebuchadnezzar's image to be worshiped are both examples of lawlessness and the Antichrist spirit. In the above scrip ture, "the man of lawlessness" is the Antichrist. That verse in King James version of the Bible he is called "the man of sin."

There was very effective communication going on in the Tower of Babel society because everyone spoke the same lan guage. Communication is an essential part of community building because the people must be able to give and receive commands to achieve a common goal. King Nebuchadnezzar's society also knew that well. They placed great systems of communication for the common goal. Daniel didn't agree with all of King Nebuchadnezzar's goals. Daniel was part of Nebuchadnezzar's society, but he didn't agree with all the commands of the king. Daniel and his three Hebrew friends got in trouble because there were some rules they were not in agreement with. What does our society have to say today that you and I as Christians are not able to agree with or conform to?

The society led by Nimrod came together to build a struc ture to go all the way up to the heavens. Does this sound familiar? Are you making a connection between what was going on in Genesis 11 and the telecom towers in your own cities? Your cell phone would not work without a tower. It takes signals from high places to enjoy these conveniences that our society has provided to us.

In a great modern-day example of Genesis 11, there was recently a rumor that Facebook created two robots that, on their own, developed their own language. If the story was true, it is obvious that they didn't trust the integrity of the robots. Later, it was said that it was an error, but I learned something, nonetheless. The creator is not comfortable with the creature overtaking its environment. It was the same sce nario as in Genesis 11. God created man—He knows what is in us and prefers to not allow us to function independently.

Is there a price for our world's technology advancing and becoming more convenient? Or maybe we should ask this question: Is Nimrod still building? Is his spirit still leading the builders of communities today? As I previously said, the spirit of Nimrod was functioning in rebellion. If his ideas had been according to the plans of God, then God would not have scattered them or their plans. But just like Adam and Eve in the garden of Eden, rebellion took over. After speaking to the serpent, Eve had an agenda of getting greater knowledge, which God was not in accord with. His command to Adam about the forbidden tree made that clear.

IT IS WRITTEN

Since the Fall of man, we have struggled with the com mandments of God. The days that we live in today do not make it easier as time progresses. But we must remember, as citizens of heaven, we are to live according to God's com mands. Daniel understood that. The way the world functions is different from the way that the Kingdom of God functions.

Jesus taught us how to live in this world and be a citizen of heaven. He would simply quote scripture each time that the devil attacked Him. He told the enemy, "It is written." In the battle of the soul that Satan took up with Eve in the garden, God's own words were Eve's only defense. The problem was that she entertained the serpent's words and arguments instead.

In our society, the same thing is going on that was in the garden of Eden. God's rules and regulations are being twisted. In fact, the word "love," as used in some societies today, can be quite evil. In some circles, when you hear the word "love" or "light," it's not the godly kind. Rather, these words are now more often associated with the new age movement. God's rules and regulations are twisted to shape and form the agendas of this world. We must not conform to the new age or the world's definition of these words. The common goal in this world is the opposite of God's way.

Each nation lives by a culture and certain customs. Each nation's individual culture or custom does not necessarily present a threat to humanity. Rather, it is the gathering of all nations for a one world government that is a problem. this will yield a governmental system that is similar to that of Nimrod and Nebuchadnezzar—a society of one world and one voice but without the Almighty Creator, God. It is a society that is in direct conflict with what God intended. That is why the kings of this world plan against God and against His anointed (Psalm 2). John warns us of being in love with the agendas of this world.

> *Love not the world, neither the things that are in the world. If any man love the world, the love of the Father is not in him. For all that is in the world, the lust of the flesh, and the lust of the eyes, and the pride of life, is not of the Father, but is of the world.*
>
> —1 John 2:15–16

As we look at the different societies and kingdoms that exist today, we are aware that they challenge us for being part of the Kingdom of God. We are not the first generation that has faced this trial. We find Noah, Lot, Daniel, Hananiah, Mishael, Azariah, the disciples, and even Jesus in that same sit uation you and I are in.

Apostle Paul says,

For though we walk in the flesh, we do not war after the flesh.

—2 Corinthians 10:3

This world is temporary for us. We have another home. We must live here as Daniel lived in Babylon. Our eyes must be fixed on our Lord Jesus Christ and the Kingdom of God. Jesus told His prosecutors that His kingdom is not of this world.

Look at the way he dealt directly with Satan:

*Then was Jesus led up of the Spirit into the wilder ness to be tempted of the devil. And when he had fasted forty days and forty nights, he was after ward an hungred. And when the tempter came to him, he said, If thou be the Son of God, com mand that these stones be made bread. But he answered and said, **It is written**, Man shall not live by bread alone, but by every word that pro ceedeth out of the mouth of God. Then the devil taketh him up into the holy city, and setteth him on a pinnacle of the temple, And saith unto him, If thou be the Son of God, cast thyself down: **for it is written**, He shall give his angels charge concerning thee: and in their hands they shall bear thee up, lest at any time thou dash thy foot against a stone. Jesus said unto him, **It is written** again, Thou shalt not tempt the Lord thy God. Again, the devil taketh him up into an exceeding high mountain, and sheweth him all the* *kingdoms of the world, and the glory of them; And saith unto him, All these things will I give thee, if thou wilt fall down and worship me. Then saith Jesus unto him, Get thee hence, Satan: **for it is written**, Thou shalt worship the Lord thy God, and him only shalt thou serve.*

—Matthew 4:1–10 (emphasis mine)

After reading this passage, I think it's safe to say that we need to know our Bibles. Knowing the Word of God will keep us from functioning in lawlessness. Daniel knew beyond a shadow of the doubt if he would simply eat God's diet, he'd be strong. In fact, he would be many times stronger than the others. David also understood if he would simply armor himself with God's armor, he'd get victory over Goliath.

My brothers and sisters, it is the same for us today. Daniel 11:32 tells us the wicked will continue in their wickedness, but those that know their God will be strong and do exploits. We are living in a day and time that we must know our God and know Him intimately. Hebrews 10:7 tells us Jesus came in the volume of a book. In Matthew 4:4, Jesus tells us that we do not live by food alone but by every word that comes from God. The words that proceed out of the mouth of God are in fact the words in the Bible and personal words that the Lord had spoken to you. The enemy cannot stand against what God says.

The difference between Eve's battle with Satan and Jesus's battle with Satan was the word exchange and knowledge of God. Eve was manipulated by the serpent with the Word of God. Jesus fought Satan with the Word of God by knowledge. Eve became a victim, but Jesus became a victor. Also in the encounters of Daniel and the Hebrew men with the Babylonians we find the same element present; they overcame their circumstances and challenges because they had knowledge of God and His Word.

And then will I profess unto them, I never knew you: depart from me, ye that work iniquity.

—Matthew 7:23

Matthew 7:23 is a reality that shakes me. It would be an unfortunate thing to hear Jesus say to me, "Away from me. I never knew you." To avoid this, I have to be one with Him. How can I be one with Him? I have to eat His flesh and drink His blood. There's a saying that says, "You are what you eat." We must be one with and know our God. How can we know Him? We must know what is written in the Word of God so we can protect our souls in today's societies. It's like eating Daniel's diet. Daniel's diet was hunger for wisdom and insight, and he was indeed filled. Daniel's diet was more than just giving up deli cious meals in the natural. It was a spiritual diet. Daniel gave his appetite to His God and not to the desires or lusts of this present life. He ate for spiritual strength instead of pleasure. His diet was connected to the principles in the Word of God. He ate as if he were eating manna, which is bread from heaven. The bread from heaven is the Word of God. Eating the Word of God will teach us, and make us strong, many times stronger than all this world's witchcraft and manipulations. In Matthew 4:4 Jesus tells us that we live by the word that comes out of God's mouth, not just by natural bread.

In the book of Proverbs, we learn the knowledge of God is the beginning of wisdom. Isaiah declares to us that God's ways and thoughts are higher than ours. That's why we must know what is written because His thoughts are written for us, and the Bible is full of His ways.

In the book of Daniel, we find that Daniel was not con formed to the Babylonian mindset. His mind was constantly washed through fasting, abiding in prayer, and by the knowledge of the Word of God.

It is clear that the mind is cleansed by the Word of God. Jesus told the disciples,

Now ye are clean through the word which I have spoken unto you.

—John 15:3

Also, Psalm 119 says,

Wherewithal shall a young man cleanse his way? by taking heed thereto according to thy word.

—Psalm 119:9

Daniel was brought in to Babylon for the very purpose of conformation but was able to stay clean in the midst of what society demanded.

MOVIES, MUSIC, AND CARTOONS IN OUR SOCIETY

Then an herald cried aloud, To you it is com manded, O people, nations, and languages, That at what time ye hear the sound of the cornet, flute, harp, sackbut, psaltery, dulcimer, and all kinds of musick, ye fall down and worship the golden image that Nebuchadnezzar the king hath set up.

—Daniel 3:4–5

Movies, music, and cartoons are used as communicators to us whether we are aware of it or not. These media are showing us that the more we are exposed to something, the easier it is to accept it no matter how evil it is. How can that be? Well, to be able to explain this, let's pay attention to what the Word of God says about this world in the times that we live in. Keep in mind also that Romans 10:17 says, *"So then faith cometh by hearing, and hearing by the word of God."*

Certainly, we know that from the very beginning, there is a society that came about that was functioning in lawless ness, in other words, without God's permission. That society is still here, and they want you and I to conform. The Bible also tells us that in the last days knowledge shall be increased. Physicists and other scientists have been studying for many, many years so that they will be able to overtake and control humanity. They use what God has created and through cal culations and manipulations and without regard to God to plan their overtake. Again, the same thing in the garden of Eden Satan overtook humanity (the world) through lawless ness. He twisted God's law. Please understand Satan did not just tell Eve to eat the fruit. Satan came with the knowledge of what God said. He was very cunning in the way that he overtook her.

Some years ago, I learned of this machine called CERN. It's the European Organization for Nuclear Research, cen tered in Switzerland, founded by about a dozen nations. It's the largest particle physics lab- oratory in the world. What does that mean? They are attempting to make intense calculations in predictions so that they are able to control humanity to even the cellular level. So you see, that is how certain predic tions can be made even with cartoons like *The Jetsons*. Don't forget, Daniel said knowledge will become great in the last days. We are living it.

Television uses cartoons, such as *The Simpsons,* that are utterly inap- propriate, to push the agenda. They take the imag ination of the child and begin to conform it to the mindset of this world. Satan understands that the mind of the child is fragile and undeveloped. Just as he went to the weaker vessel in the garden of Eden, he goes after the children. Even in the time of the captivity in Babylon, he called for the young minds to be brought forth to be molded for the agenda.

Movies are no different. It is also difficult to find a movie that is not challenging to the mind even of the adult. And television is described it as a medium to "tell a vision." But what vision? It is the vision that the man of lawlessness sees for humanity. That is the danger we are in. The man of per dition or the man of sin wants to tell us or show us what he would want of us. It's no different from the garden of Eden or from the time of Judah's captivity.

Music is another major medium that Satan uses to send his messages to us, and it's possibly the most dangerous one. Music demands your body, soul, and spirit. It tends to move you and touches all the emotions of the human being. It can reach and touch a part of the soul that can last for a lifetime. This is why music is used in learning and therapy. But it is also why it is used in just about every store that you will walk into to influence your shopping, and it is used by the gov ernment, even as it was used by King Nebuchadnezzar. The king played music, and his subjects were to bow down to the sound. In churches, we use music to worship God, but Satan also understands the power of music. King Saul needed music to appease his demons.

Music and movie stars of this world sell their souls to Satan for fame, and they become a medium to speak through. It is unfortunate to say that music, movies, and cartoons can turn us into puppets. What do I mean by that? I have learned that some crimes are committed after some listen to a certain album. The reason is because the sounds give boldness to perform the act. Also, the messages that are in music, movies, and cartoons many times suggest participation in sin.

Satan's plan is to tear down God's original creation. Humanity is the most important creation to God—that's what this is all about. Society says it's okay to be confused about your sexuality. I'm not sure how it is in other nations, but I know in the United States, parents are fighting laws about the sexuality of their children. Even in the schools, they are teaching the children that it's okay to be a different gender than God made them to be. Our news broadcasts, social media, movies, music and TV shows promote these agendas. These media are constantly presenting visuals that are con troversial to God's original plan of male and female. This has brought forth a lot of confusion to children and parents alike.

We must remember that the name of Babylon comes from the word *babel*, which means confusion. Social media, the news broadcast channels, movies, and so on are all places that don't lack babbling. They influence our societies by inserting or babbling the world's ultimate agenda into our souls. We must not have an appetite for their insight and agenda. Daniel had an appetite for God's insight. I heard a physicist say, "One day we will eventually get complete inde pendence from humans." How can we possibly think that a human and a robot can have a baby, but scientists in society today are working on that exact thing. The media are pushing these agendas wisely, slowly, and surely, even as Satan pushed his agenda with Eve wisely. Television have been working on the human psyche for very many years, preparing them to take the bite.

CALLING EVIL GOOD AND GOOD EVIL

Isaiah 5:20 prophesied that people will call evil good and good evil. How sad is it that we frown on the killing of ani mals but accept killing babies? There are companies that will allow all reading materials except Bibles. Why would we fight for a boy to be a girl and a girl to be a boy?

We serve a holy God. One thing we are sure of is that the Kingdom of God is different from any other kingdom on earth. After man's Fall, Jesus brought the opportunity to receive God's kingdom on the earth. Jesus came preaching, "The kingdom of God is at hand." That's the gospel! God has a king, and His name is Jesus. In His kingdom, there are rules and regulations.

What God says is not what this world says. The evil one always has something opposite to say. You must keep in mind the devil comes to kill and to destroy. Isaiah 14 and Ezekiel 28 tell of the fall of Satan. He roams the earth looking for those he can devour. He's not able to devour everyone, so he has to find those that are vulnerable. The Bible calls him the deceiver, the accuser of the brethren. Jesus called him the father of lies. Lucifer was the cherub and covering angel, but he has fallen.

In 2 Corinthians 4:4, Satan is called the god of this world. This is the god Daniel experienced as being over Babylon. He lived in a world or society whose god was not the God he knew and served. Interestingly enough though, kings like Nebuchadnezzar who were a type of a god to the people would confess the sovereignty of Daniel's God, the God who is truly the God of all gods.

With this flawed perception, we are all able to see why society's view is different from God's view. What God says is not what society says. This world's vision is not in line with our God's vision. Its viewpoint is not truth and holiness or godly love. Its agenda is influenced and even dedicated to the father of lies. The name of the game here on earth is lawless ness, which is to call evil good and good evil.

Therefore, Jesus had to overcome the temptations of the flesh with the reply "It is written." The laws of God stand to give life. Adam and Eve could have learned a lesson from that encounter between Jesus and Satan in Matthew 4. In fact, if Adam and Eve would have had the same understanding as Jesus, we would not have been subject to this god of this world today. Selah!

It's amazing how easy it is to twist the Word of God. It's so subtle to call evil good and good evil. In fact, it may even make you feel guilty that you're calling something bad while society is saying it's good. An example would be love, the way that the word is used or maybe what it is. The world tells us that two people of the same sex can love each other in a sexual way, and our society makes you feel wrong to think or say that it is wrong. The Word of God calls it wrong. Clearly, God made man and woman to engage in sexual activity in marriage.

Another example is the deep love that people sometimes have for their pets in comparison to actual people. I person ally know someone who said they'd kill a person if they hurt their pet snake. Wait a minute! Would you kill a human being made in God's image for a pet? I certainly don't agree that a pet should be hurt, but to consider taking a human life is a bit extreme. Evil called good.

CHAPTER SEVEN

REMEMBER DANIEL'S PROPHESY

When ye therefore shall see the abomination of desolation, spoken of by Daniel the prophet, stand in the holy place, (whoso readeth, let him understand).

—Matthew 24:15

THIS IS ONE of the greatest prophecies in all the Bible—the prophecy of the second coming of Jesus Christ. Why? In earlier chapters we established that Daniel speaks over a time span that stretches from the captivity of Jerusalem to the return of Jesus Christ. That makes the book of Daniel a pretty important book. We must pay attention to the message that God is giving us through his book.

His book is about as important as the book of Revelation. Revelation 1:3 states, "Blessed is he that reads and hears the words of this prophecy."

That's how important the book of Revelation is. It's the only book in the holy Bible that makes such a promise. I call the book of Daniel and the book of Revelation brothers because they are connected in several ways. They are both packed with the prophetic.

I am so grateful to God for the book of Daniel. In Daniel I find the character I must have to live by and endure during the "time of the end." The time of the end will be a time of captivity for many, but even as Daniel proves, we don't all have to live in complete captivity. I believe that this is one of the main lessons of the book. Daniel's focus was not on the governmental system of this world. The Kingdom of God is a spiritual government system, and that's where he focused himself to live—in God's spiritual government system.

As Jesus spoke to His disciples about the end of all things and His return He said, "…when ye see"

My question to our generation is: What do you see? Or rather, Are you even able to see? There are more questions that should be asked, in fact Do you see? Can we see? Sounds to me like here through Jesus's tone, He is expecting you and I to see. He didn't say, "if "; He said, "when." The sad thing is, God says plainly in His Word in Hosea 4:6 that His people perish for lack of knowledge He is aware that there will be some that will perish because they don't know; they don't see That should not be you or me because we are getting the knowledge Let's just be sure that we don't reject the knowledge.

AND THIS GOSPEL OF THE KINGDOM SHALL BE PREACHED… AND THEY THAT UNDERSTAND AMONG THE PEOPLE SHALL INSTRUCT MANY

> *And this gospel of the kingdom shall be preached in all the world for a witness unto all nations; and then shall the end come. When ye therefore shall see the abomination of desola-*

tion, spoken of by Daniel the prophet, stand in the holy place,
(whoso readeth, let him understand:)

—Matthew 24:14–15

And such as do wickedly against the covenant shall he corrupt
by flatteries: but the people that do know their God shall be
strong, and do exploits. And they that understand among the
people shall instruct many: yet they shall fall by the sword,
and by flame, by captivity, and by spoil, many days.

—Daniel 11:32–33

I believe the time of the second coming of Jesus Christ is approaching very quickly. In fact, that is my urgency and pur pose for writing this book. I remember the Sunday morning that the Lord instructed me to write this book. This book is a warning for those who want to see and understand. We must pay attention to what we should be doing.

Both Jesus and Daniel tell us what we should be doing. Daniel 11:32 and 33 expose a harsh reality of each individ ual's place. This is not the time to judge what the wicked are doing. Let's understand they will do what they are called to do. Rather, let's focus on what we should be doing. In the days of Noah the wicked were very wicked and living their best lives, but Noah was focused on building an ark in prepara tion for salvation.

During this end time we need to get to know God better to do exploits. That is what Daniel is pointing out that will happen with the people of God in that season. He also points out that those that have knowledge will instruct the others.

Matthew 24 is generally known as the end-time chapter. It's the chapter where Jesus gave information of the end times. Right before Jesus spoke about Daniel's prophecy concerning the end times, He pointed out we should be busy preaching the gospel. Yes, the good news must be preached so the world can get an opportunity to enter in.

As we examine this message of Matthew 24 in its fullness, it's important that we pay attention to the words of Jesus con cerning His return. One of the signs of Jesus's return is the preaching of the gospel of the Kingdom of God. Notice Jesus said, "This gospel." The word "gospel" generally means good news. I believe he said, "This" because he was speaking to the disciples and was emphasizing the gospel that he was teaching them. Jesus was making a point of which gospel needed to be preached. Evidence of that is to see how many religious groups there are today. Jesus wanted them to understand that in the last days there would be many gospels or religions. We must be very careful during this time to be sure that the gospel that is being preached is this same gospel that Jesus was speaking about: the gospel of Jesus Christ, which is the kingdom of God. It's the only way to the Father. Jesus came preaching, "The kingdom is at hand." Making this point is important because there will be a lot of false kingdoms, false religions, even false christs preached during the end time. Jesus made that clear also in verses 23 and 24 of the chapter.

Just to clarify, because students have asked me this ques tion, there is no real difference between the gospel of Jesus Christ and the Kingdom of God. The Father and the son are one. The gospel of Jesus Christ would be the good news about Jesus's work on the cross for our salvation. The kingdom of God is God's government and His reign. I believe Jesus is using the language "this gospel of the kingdom" because we must be mindful to preach about His kingdom—the coming King and His reign. The battle in this world during the last days has to do with the kingdom of this world trying to over take you and I for itself.

God's kingdom is an alternative and in fact the best pick between those two kingdoms. Thank God for that option! Many will choose the kingdom of the Antichrist and enter into everlasting hell fire. To under- stand this best, we must understand what the kingdom is. A kingdom is simply a ter ritory ruled by a king. In our case, the King is Jesus.

Humanity will need to hear the option of falling under the rule of the kingdom of God versus the society or the earthly kingdom at the end time. Once the man of sin sets up his reign, then people must know that the reign of Jesus Christ is the alternative and that He, the true King, is on His way. We must preach that people cannot lose hope in the coming Kingdom of God because many will be fooled by the setup of the Antichrist, which will be the abomination of desolation standing in the holy place. Jesus Christ is the only one that has the right to stand in such a holy place. So we must tell people not to be misled and sit under the Antichrist's lordship.

Apostle Paul in 1 Thessalonians 5:3 warned, "Or when they shall say, Peace and safety; then sudden destruction cometh upon them, as travail upon a woman with child; and they shall not escape." We must tell the world what is going on, but first we must see for ourselves. The times will be terrible, but they will say and falsely offer peace and safety. You that are wise will know the truth. It's time to preach. Sound the alarm!

A great example of the gospel being preached right before the coming of the Lord is found in Matthew 25. It reads,

> *And at midnight there was a cry made, Behold, the bridegroom cometh; go ye out to meet him.*

> —Matthew 25:6

This is intense because you hear the urgency of the preaching as a cry. There is such emotional intensity attached to the preaching of the gospel of Jesus Christ in the end times as it is such a serious period. The destiny of souls are hanging on the line. Apostle Paul tells us,

> *This know also, that in the last days perilous times shall come.*

> —2 Timothy 3:1

Those final days on earth will be a time of absolute difficulty, terror, and peril. The world will need to hear, with urgency. They will need to hear there's another option for them. We need strong preaching of the gospel. Just like in the parable of the ten virgins in Matthew 25, there was noise in the city saying the bridegroom is coming. Could that noise be a revival? I believe so. The evidence of revival in the end times is found in the great harvest of souls in Revelation 14. This chapter is positioned right after the mark of the beast is spoken of in Revelation 13. Great harvest is usually the fruit of great revivals. A revival is needed in this hour for the Church to realize the time is near. We don't know the exact time, but we've been given clues and warnings about the hour. We must be prepared and prepare souls for the time of that great harvest. Matthew 25 is a parable given by Jesus, which follows the chapter where He gives us the signs, warnings, and insights of the last days.

It's important to hear the parables that he ties to the chapters after his teaching on the end times. He is telling us what the end-time Church will be like. We must pay attention to the slumber and the cry as well as the lack of oil. If people are sleeping and not paying attention, they will not be aware of the Antichrist as he sets up his reign. This will cause many in the Church to be deceived. Therefore, the gospel of the end time must be preached and taught everywhere.

...In All the World...

All the world needs to hear of the gospel of Jesus Christ. Since Genesis chapter 11, humanity have had a plan to become great. Unfortunately, there had to be a great divide because their agenda was against God, the Creator of man. Man's big ideas to become great without God's permission will never stand. The man Nimrod was the leader of the operation of the Tower of Babel.

The word "Babylon" comes from the root word "babel," which actually means "many confusing voices." The word "baal" is the Hebrew word for master or even owner. It's a spirit that still tempts the world to be its own master and leave the Creator out. But when they're not able to do it them selves they get rewards from another lord. Humanity was scattered by God over the face of the earth to stop the wicked plan that man devised with Satan's help.

According to Ephesians 1:4, He had a plan of reconcilia tion for us even before the divide. God has a plan to bring us all back to Him. The plan of salvation is God's great love for us.

> *And I saw another angel fly in the midst of heaven, having the everlasting gospel to preach unto them that dwell on the earth, and to every nation, and kindred, and tongue, and people....*

—Revelation 14:6

In Mark, Jesus gave us what most call "the Great Commission." It reads,

> *And he said unto them, Go ye into all the world, and preach the gospel to every creature.*

—Mark 16:15

He said to "all the world" and to "every creature." Many missionaries stand on this passage for their lives' work. The gospel must be preached to all nations because the glory of all nations will be in heaven according to Revelation:

> *And they shall bring the glory and honour of the nations into it.*

—Revelation 21:26

...*For a Witness unto All Nations*...

Normally, a witness is a person who was present and saw something occur. This person will bring evident proof of the happening. In other words, it is a person that can agree with or confirm something. For example, witnesses go into court and testify. In this case, however, it's an action. Jesus is telling us in this passage that the preaching all over the world will be used as witness to bring evidence for judgment unto all nations of this earth. This is why we must preach. For what God wants to do, this witness must be present. The wit ness is our act of preaching the gospel. The world must say amen to their punishment because our preaching will speak against them if they reject. Jesus tells his 12 disciples this as he sends them out.

In Acts 1 before His ascension, Jesus specifically told his disciples to be witnesses unto him. His last instructions to them were those few words. God's complete plan included their equipping to do the job. He did not only tell them to be a witness but also told them that they would need to be empowered, and He gave them direction on how to accom plish this.

This is one of the reasons we are paying attention to Daniel. Obviously, Daniel had something that caused him to be empowered to live during that time of intense captivity because he was a great witness. His life preached because he lived a powerful life. Daniel caused wicked kings to fall on their knees because of his anointing. The Holy Spirit is God's provision for us. Before Jesus's ascension, He provided the power so we may be a witness unto Him.

> *But ye shall receive power, after that the Holy Ghost is come upon you: and ye shall be wit nesses unto me both in Jerusalem, and in all Judaea, and in Samaria, and unto the uttermost part of the earth.*

> —Acts 1:8

In this verse, Jesus was answering the disciples' question about the timing of the restoration of the Kingdom. He was indeed talking about the end times. Jesus was aware that we would need power to do the work of the kingdom for the full restoration between God and humanity.

The disciples were actually asking Jesus about the timing of His return, restoration of the Kingdom. Jesus altogether ignores their curiosity and tells them it's not their business, it's the Father's deal. And instead, he points them to the direction of receiving the power that will take for them to do the work of the ministry. We must be empowered to be a witness of the gospel in this end time.

The life of Daniel taught us about the price for the anointing that must come to be able to withstand the oppo sition this world's system. We must receive power so that we can say no to this system and also be a witness to those that need us.

The power of the Holy Spirit is what will help us to be the witness that we need to be unto all the nations. Daniel would not have been able to withstand the lions without that consecrated life that he lived. Meshach, Shadrach, and Abednego would have bent their knees to the sound of the music and the mage if they were not empowered by a life of fasting and prayer. These were powerful witnesses unto the Babylonian kingdom. Daniel and his friends' confession of their God did not go unnoticed. Kings were impressed and confessed that the God of Israel was the God of gods. This witness will judge them on that great day. God is asking this witness of us as well.

...And Then Shall the End Come

This is the event that centuries have been waiting for—the end. Jesus says no one knows the day nor the hour. One thing for sure, though, we are expected to know the signs. Jesus gave us so many clues about the end times that He expects us to know. He calls those that are not on watch "hypocrites" in Matthew:

And in the morning, It will be foul weather to day: for the sky is red and lowering. O ye hypo crites, ye can discern the face of the sky; but can ye not discern the signs of the times?

—Matthew 16:3

I would say He expects us to know the signs of the times! Even the 10 women are described as wise or foolish in the parable of the virgins in Matthew 25. I believe Jesus is dis turbed, not because we don't know, but because we prefer not to know. Some people would rather live their lives just as in the days of Noah.

According to the parable of the 10 virgins in Matthew 25, the end will be at a very dark hour. The passion week, which is also known as "the holy week," was the last week of Jesus's life on earth. As we read the gospels it is obvious that it was a difficult time for Jesus's disciples. So will it be also for the Church in the last seven years at the end time. It will be a time of great tribulation and much bloodshed. When it was all over with, Jesus simply said, *"It is finished,"* and He gave up the ghost. Where did the ghost go? It went up to the Father even as the Church shall go up to the Father. Here are these words in **John 19:30** that say, *"When Jesus therefore had received the vinegar, he said, It is finished: and he bowed his head, and gave up the ghost."* We find another passage of scripture that is very similar. It is in **Revelation 21:6** He said, "It is done." This is Jesus speaking again; how ever, this time He is speaking of the end of the world. There is a relationship with His departure from the earth and the Church's departure from this earth. Do you see it?

WHEN YE THEREFORE SHALL SEE THE ABOMINATION OF DESOLATION...

I imagine these words mean we must be paying attention. Timing and seeing are both important here.

In the book of Daniel, the first verse points out timing. There is a set time for this event to happen. Right now we are in the year of 2023. God goes into great lengths to tell us what has been coming for thousands of years. The Bible details this subject of the end times even to the point of years and weeks, though we are not given an exact date. God just wants us to pay attention. People have been guessing the date for decades or longer, but Jesus specifically says to look for "the abomination of desolation." This means we must get a good understanding of what this is so we can recognize it when it comes.

The abomination of desolation is associated with the Antichrist standing in the holy place and claiming to hold the sovereignty of God. This is an outrage because only God is God. The abomination is known to be pagan sacrifices in the Jewish temple. Like the tower of Babel, this cannot stand for long.

Matthew 24:15 leaves us with a thought. It says, "whoso readeth let him understand." These words in the parenthesis of the verse are more of a question to the reader like, "Do you understand?" I feel the writer is telling us we must get an understanding of what is being said. Many scholars have worked on this question to get an understanding. There are several different opinions on this verse. From what we can gather, it will be "standing" in the holy place. The word "standing" here gives us an indication that it will be a setup. The word "abomination" means a thing that is detestable and causes disgust. What is the most detestable thing to our God? Idolatry. The word desolation means great despair and sadness. That tells me there will be great darkness coming from that setup in the holy place during that time.

After much research of different libraries, books, and other scholars I sum it up this way. The abomination of desolation is Lucifer himself, the same devil that embodied the serpent in Eden, who influenced Nimrod, and whom Nebuchadnezzar served that will be set up and ruling in the holy place as if he were God. His ruling in the holy place is not only an abomination but will bring forth desolation, chaos, and perilous times for mankind. It will be a horrific setup.

...SPOKEN OF BY DANIEL THE PROPHET...

Jesus was the greatest prophet that ever lived. It's a big deal when the greatest prophet that ever lived refers you to another prophet's work. Jesus confirmed the prophetic gift of Daniel, almost as if to say to him, "Well done, good and faithful servant."

As I read these words that Jesus spoke, I feel that every jot and every tittle is important. It may seem tedious to look at every word in this phrase, but the Bible commands us to get a clear understanding. Somehow, I believe the Lord is saying something deep here. Our souls are on the line, and there's something we need to see. The prophet Daniel has a key for our lives in this day and time.

The word "spoken" is an utterance in the past tense. What does the Bible tell us about speaking? God spoke at the Creation to create. The Bible also tells us that man lives by what comes out of the mouth of God. Daniel was one of God's mouthpieces. God use prophets to say what He wants to tell us. The spoken Word of God through His chosen vessels is powerful. Think of it.

...STAND IN THE HOLY PLACE...

Jesus describes the abomination of desolation as standing. We find this false trinity in Revelation 13. The dragon, the beast, and the Antichrist will be in that holy place. I believe that stand means established or set up. Daniel was a man of vision, and he could see. Can you and I? What did Jesus mean when He said, "He who has an ear to hear let him hear."? He was talking about us opening our spiritual ears. For this grand event that He is referring to in Matthew, we need spiritual eyes. This is serious stuff. I believe we need to pay attention to Daniel's lifestyle so we can see as he saw.

This establishment (the stand) will cause persecutions like in Daniel's day. The days will be dark and evil, loveless. From the stand of the false trinity in the holy place, there will be decrees of sentences to lions' dens and fiery furnaces for Christians for their righteous living. Others will be persecuted for not bowing down to society's demands. Don't be surprised when you begin to see more fires in certain nations in the streets. These are manifestations and phenomena from the plan of the enemy.

...(WHOSO READETH, LET HIM UNDERSTAND)...

Now is the time to understand the end time. As you read this book, I pray you understand. When the Lord speaks of things that are serious or difficult, He likes to add special attention to them so we can take a deeper look. After He tells us this great truth about the end times, we are instructed not just to read it but to be sure to pay close attention so we understand it. The Lord knew our eternity depended on it. I believe our eternity depends on the information that we are getting in this book.

The end-time remnant is a special group of people, a Daniel generation. We must be strong to endure to the end. The subject of the end times is all over the Bible. God says that His people perish for lack of knowledge. This end-time remnant must be able to see, hear, and understand: we must be able to see the abomination of desolation. We must be able to hear the trumpet. We must be able to understand the hour. Know your God and do exploits!

www.ingramcontent.com/pod-product-compliance
Lightning Source LLC
Chambersburg PA
CBHW071009120626
46546CB00003B/1008